LITERACY LEADERSHIP
TO SUPPORT READING IMPROVEMENT

Literacy Leadership
to Support Reading Improvement

Intervention Programs and Balanced Instruction

Mary Kay Moskal
Ayn F. Keneman

THE GUILFORD PRESS
New York   London

© 2011 The Guilford Press
A Division of Guilford Publications, Inc.
72 Spring Street, New York, NY 10012
www.guilford.com

Printed in the United States of America

This book is printed on acid-free paper.

Last digit is print number: 9 8 7 6 5 4 3 2 1

Library of Congress Cataloging-in-Publication Data
Moskal, Mary Kay.
  Literacy leadership to support reading improvement : intervention programs and balanced instruction / Mary Kay Moskal, Ayn F. Keneman.
      p. cm.
  Includes bibliographical references and index.
  ISBN 978-1-60918-487-2 (pbk. : alk. paper) — ISBN 978-1-60918-488-9 (hardcover : alk. paper)
  1. Reading—Remedial teaching.   I. Keneman, Ayn F.   II. Title.
  LB1050.5.M685 2011
  372.41′4—dc23
                                                                2011022376

For Camille
Our teacher, our mentor, our friend

About the Authors

Mary Kay Moskal, EdD, is Associate Professor of Reading and Language Arts in the Kalmanovitz School of Education at Saint Mary's College of California in Moraga. She is Co-Director of the Literacy Learning Clinic and a past president of the Organization of Teacher Educators in Reading (OTER), a special interest group of the International Reading Association. Dr. Moskal is coauthor, with Camille Blachowicz, of the book *Partnering for Fluency.*

Ayn F. Keneman, EdD, is Associate Professor of Elementary and Middle Level Education in the National College of Education at National-Louis University in Chicago. She teaches reading and language courses for the Academy of Urban School Leadership, a partnership with the Chicago Public Schools and National-Louis. Dr. Keneman is a past president of the Illinois Young Authors' Conference.

Preface

One hundred years from now, it will not matter what kind of car
I drove, what kind of house I lived in, or how much money I had
in the bank, but the world may be a better place because I made
a difference in a child's life.

—AUTHOR UNKNOWN

Reading makes a difference in a student's life, and with reading life is better. We've
seen this difference with the students we've taught. It happened when Adam picked up a
Maurice Sendak book and realized he could "really read" *on his own*. It happened when
Isabel first read a book just because she *wanted* to, which resulted in reading a whole
series of books simply for pleasure. And although *Literacy Leadership to Support Reading
Improvement: Intervention Programs and Balanced Instruction* is written for leaders in
literacy, it is ultimately written to benefit children and young adults so reading can make
a difference in their lives.

The literacy lives of elementary, middle, and high school readers have been important to us for years. Beginning in 1992, we were both part of a group of four women,
all literacy leaders, who regularly met and discussed the reading needs of students. We
pushed each other's thinking and deepened our understandings of what it meant to be a
reader and what it meant to read well. Our conversation topics varied, but we usually discussed how to improve reading instruction and help those who struggled with the task of
reading. Mary Kay's move to the West Coast in 2002 meant that the meetings occurred
less frequently, but the passion for supporting reading improvement stayed strong.

This book is a result of that passion. In our current work at National-Louis University and Saint Mary's College of California, we've had opportunities to work with
exemplary literacy leaders who created reading intervention programs and excellent
balanced instruction to assist readers in elementary, middle, and high schools. To support or supplement the teachers' use of state- or district-selected reading curriculum in

their schools, literacy leaders described in these chapters have implemented different approaches to promote reading success with specific student populations and in school-wide contexts. We share their stories and programs so that you can replicate or implement similar designs and innovations for the benefit of any reader who may need assistance. Deshler, Deshler, and Biancarosa (2007) express the need for a book like this, offering a collection of successful reading approaches and programs that—as a result of dedicated literacy educators—have become an integral part of a school community.

Literacy leaders and leadership are addressed throughout the book. We define literacy leaders as educators who implement and guide others in implementing research-based literacy practices in schools. They are committed to supporting teachers and staff based on the needs of the student population, and they have a vision for building active learning based on a solid understanding of teaching for both adults and children (Lyons & Pinnell, 2001). These educational leaders could be teachers, reading specialists, literacy coaches, curriculum directors, literacy coordinators, and administrators with current in-depth knowledge of literacy.

These are the same literacy leaders we see as our audience. This book offers instruction and programs that were found to be successful and have made a difference in the reading education of students. As literacy leaders ourselves, we see the value of the intervention programs and balanced instruction described here because (1) they have been implemented in naturalistic settings, (2) they are based on theory and research, and (3) they have resulted in reading improvement.

The book is organized into three main parts. Part I, Literacy Leadership to Support Struggling Readers, lays the foundations for the book and then examines reading improvement focusing on struggling readers. Those who struggle are failing to master reading practices and need the right instruction to allow them to acquire and practice skills and strategies effectively. When they are successful, they are motivated to continue to learn, even when reading tasks are demanding.

Chapter 1 details the critical importance of effective reading and how literacy leaders conceptualize reading improvement through balanced instruction and research-based interventions. Two case studies, of a fourth grader and a sixth grader, highlight some of these struggles in context. The chapter looks at assumptions about learning by examining theory and school mission statements and concludes with an overview of balanced reading instruction.

Chapter 2 highlights an exemplary implementation of response to intervention (RTI) in one elementary school. It explains how the school is breaking the cycle of frustration and failure felt by first graders by implementing a collaborative model that focuses on the child's needs and promotes learning for everyone. Successful implementation of RTI is discussed in the areas of school leadership, a community of learners, assessment, progress monitoring, tiered instruction, and parental engagement.

Chapter 3 describes reading interventions developed for students at risk of reading failure who need additional support. One such intervention is a districtwide 30-minute program for small groups of first and second graders. The second intervention described is an after-school reading clinic housed in an elementary school. Steps for literacy leaders to consider when creating an intervention program are shared, along with suggestions for lesson planning, assessing, and communicating with parents and classroom teachers.

Part II, Literacy Leadership with Specific Student Groupings, focuses on three different student populations who have unique difficulties with reading. Boys and literacy are examined in Chapter 4. Research on boy readers is provided, along with ways for literacy leaders to help them get excited about reading, to recommend "guys read" books (Sczieska, 2003), and to implement reading strategies that engage boys (and girls!). Approaches for reading in content areas and using digital literacies are suggested.

Chapter 5 highlights a reading class designed for middle school students who were not confident readers. The facilitation of learning in this class ultimately created a community of students who love books. The chapter provides an overview of the 3-hour literacy block program facilitated by reading and special education teachers to support and motivate struggling readers. Research shows that students need teachers to be interested in their lives, to be fair, and to involve them in learning (Johnston & Nichols, 1995; Sergiovanni, 1994), and the teachers of this program are interested, fair, and involved. The chapter also highlights the reading partnership created between the middle school students and senior members of the community who love books.

Chapter 6 focuses on one district's efforts to institutionalize literacy instruction in the content areas among their high school teachers. Initially begun to improve academic literacy and reading skills, the reform developed into a multifaceted program. Six major parts of the program are outlined, and the way in which it was integrated into the district's middle and high schools is explained. The chapter concludes with research that supports the reform and the reasons for its long-term success.

Part III, Literacy Leadership in Schoolwide Contexts, examines how literacy leaders implement reading support not only in classrooms but across the school. Through schoolwide literacy programs and instruction, the teaching community develops shared knowledge and goals for reading success that benefit all students. Chapter 7 highlights how technology, when embedded into the reading curriculum naturally, motivates and engages all learners. By examining the integration of technology into the curriculum in one elementary school, the chapter explores the challenging role of the teacher in this time of rapid change. Class lessons that include the authentic use of the SMART board, iPod Touches, individual computers, and Internet search engines are discussed.

Chapter 8 looks at how literacy leaders build partnerships among school, parents, and community. It describes a school in which family literacy workshops, developed specifically for a diverse community, were implemented to help families build literacy at home and feel welcome at school. The process of creating, implementing, and evaluating the literacy workshops is detailed. The chapter explains how partnerships can help families to support learning at school, while the school also supports learning for the parents. Research for building productive partnerships is shared.

Chapter 9 shares the steps for planning, facilitating, evaluating, and extending professional development for schoolwide change. Although written specifically for literacy leaders who have never facilitated a professional development session, experienced presenters may benefit from the content as well. The importance of professional development and a brief background on adult learning are presented. Then, with examples from literacy leader advisors, the chapter details the entire process from selecting a topic to supporting colleagues beyond the professional development session.

Each chapter in the book begins with a case example "event" to introduce the intervention program or balanced instruction, followed by the research, planning, and implementation of the program or instructional approach. Assessment and outcomes are provided when appropriate, along with reproducible examples or templates. Each chapter ends by revisiting the key ideas for implementing the interventions and instruction, along with concluding thoughts.

We invite you to read on and learn about intervention programs, balanced reading instruction, and passionate literacy leaders committed to teaching reading. We encourage you to apply the information in the chapters to your schools and students to develop programs and instruction that will make reading the difference in students' lives.

MARY KAY MOSKAL
AYN F. KENEMAN

Acknowledgments

This book contains stories and lessons from literacy leaders who are making a difference in the lives of children and young adults. We offer special thanks to all of these specialists who were so generous in allowing us to share their work with a wide audience. You are all exceptional educators.

We would also like to acknowledge the teaching and administrative staffs that welcomed us into their school communities. So many professionals took time out of their busy days to talk about various aspects of literacy, curriculum, and teaching. We are humbled by your dedication and passion.

We are deeply indebted to our editor at The Guilford Press, Craig Thomas, for his support, guidance, and patience (especially his patience!) during the writing of this book. We would also like to thank Mary Beth Wood, who assisted us in bringing everything together, making sure there were no loose ends, and Anna Nelson, who has an eye for detail and a passion for perfection. We agree that the assistance you all provided was more than we could have ever hoped for!

Sincere gratitude and appreciation go to our understanding family members (Richard, Victor, Margaret, Ellie, and Alexander) who supported us every step of the way. We are grateful for your kindness and consideration while we worked at our computers. Mary Kay would especially like to thank her family for waiting until she could join them to see the new Harry Potter movie, and Ayn would especially like to thank her husband for early-morning pots of coffee and her daughters for late-night talks on the phone.

Finally, we would like to thank you, our readers, for believing in the power of good teachers of reading. Your efforts both in and out of the classroom truly make a difference in the lives of students.

Contents

PART I

LITERACY LEADERSHIP TO SUPPORT STRUGGLING READERS

CHAPTER ONE

Reading and Literacy Leaders

If you can read this, thank a teacher.
—ANONYMOUS

It is mid-August. Educators are preparing to teach their classes, and students are preparing for another year of learning. They are excited and yet a little apprehensive, wondering what the year will bring.

Ms. Ryen is also excited but apprehensive. She is starting her second year as a reading specialist in the elementary school where she taught in the primary grades for 4 years. She thinks about the various reading strategies she implemented with the school's teachers and students the year before to help improve the students' reading skills. She felt satisfied with the relationships she was able to establish and nurture with the teachers and students as well as the mentoring program she started with the help of the neighboring middle school. This year she wants to use her better honed leadership skills to implement more reading support activities.

Down the street, Mrs. Straker surveys the list of students enrolled in her sixth-grade English and reading class. Naturally, some of these students will be average readers, and others will be above-average. Some will struggle, while a few will be at risk of failing. One might even be unable to read at all! Mrs. Straker thinks about the ways that she can best support all of her students. She knows that there are several alternatives available in her school to help the students who may find themselves struggling with their reading tasks.

Meanwhile, Mrs. Straker's former student Tom reflects about his own prospects for the seventh grade and wonders which of his friends will be in his classes. Mostly, he thinks about how he struggled with reading in school and especially when doing his homework for Mrs. Straker's sixth-grade English and reading class. When he began sixth grade, he usually couldn't remember what he had just read, but Mrs. Straker helped him improve during class. She also urged him to join the after-school homework group as well as a monthly book club and to volunteer to help mentor children in reading at the elementary school a few blocks from his middle school. Because he ended up participating in these programs, Tom was able to put into frequent practice the strategies and tools he learned about in class and after school to help him fully comprehend and remember what he had just finished reading. It took a lot of work, but it was well worth it! All in all, he feels that he is ready for a productive seventh-grade year.

Ms. Ryen, Mrs. Straker, and Tom are all part of a local school community that purposefully implements instructional supports for all aspiring readers. These supports help those who struggle both frequently or only occasionally. Some supports are extended to any students who want to participate, and some are by invitation only. Some mainly involve repeated practice by students, while others are implemented by teachers or community volunteers. But all of these supports are intended to assure that students are given the tools they need to succeed in learning to read and write well.

This book describes individuals and communities of literacy leaders, like Ms. Ryen and Mrs. Straker, whose dedicated efforts year after year contribute to creating schoolwide systems to provide reading support. These teachers realized that by moving beyond the literacy needs of their own classrooms to include the needs of the school or district, students, whether needing temporary help or long-term interventions, would gain from increased reading activities and assistance (Burns, 1999; Gunning, 2009). Supplying creativity, skill, knowledge, and ingenuity, the literacy leaders who share their endeavors in this book do so in the hope that others will repeat what they have done to create systems, projects, and programs that focus on schoolwide reading performance to the benefit of all students.

We spent additional time and have taught in schools where this approach to reading improvement was the norm. We have seen and worked with many literacy leaders who developed school programs to help with the reading difficulties of both effective and at-risk readers, and our goal in this volume is to share their stories with you. But before doing that, we can usefully examine the fundamental knowledge from which literacy leaders build their programs. This knowledge base primarily relates to the fundamentals underlying the task of reading, readers' struggles, assumptions about learning, and balanced reading instruction.

THE TASK OF READING

Often cited in the literature on reading research, E. B. Huey (1908/1968) once perceptively observed that "to completely analyze what we do when we read would almost be the acme of a psychologist's achievements, for it would be to describe some of the most intricate workings of the human mind" (p. 8). The process of reading is very complex, as Huey helped demonstrate and illustrate. He published the first thorough summarization of reading research in 1908, and this classic work continues to be referenced frequently. Huey studied reading by considering the relationship between eye movements and the brain, focusing on what he called visual cues, namely, specific letters, sounds, and words. His work was considered a landmark at the time, since he was able to show that a reader's eyes did not move smoothly across the page but rather moved and then paused in quick succession (Reed & Meyer, 2007).

Huey's (1908/1968) insights help most when considering one's intentions when reading. He observed that reading's chief aim is comprehension, that is, the goal of a proficient reader is to create meaning, not necessarily relying solely on visual "cues." Huey realized that readers use imaging and inner speech to assist in their understanding, describing them as persons who predict, calling these predictions "expectations." He explained that fluency rates vary, depending on the alertness of the reader, his or her prior knowledge of the topic being read, the reader's relative ability to concentrate, and the strategies he or she used to assist in understanding. Furthermore, he observed that health issues—for example, a lack of sleep—could impinge on the ability to read and that such matters as glare and the size of the print could also affect the reading task (Reed & Meyer, 2007).

Huey (1908/1968) built the foundation for much of what is known about reading today. Reading, as it is described in research now, is the ability to decode symbols to create words, pronounce those words, and make sense of the words alone and in various combinations, thereby leading to understanding. However, that definition is much too simplistic. The Literacy Dictionary (Harris & Hodges, 1995) includes numerous lengthy definitions of *read*, *reading*, and *comprehension*, noting that "most significantly, since reading is a learned process, definitions of reading reflect differing assumptions about learning" (p. 206). We examine some basic assumptions about learning later in this chapter.

Learning to read takes place both in and out of school—wherever children participate in either skill-based (i.e., instructional) reading or authentic (real-life) activities. The teaching of reading should be approached by using many methods, because not all children learn to read well by means of the same instructional method, but more importantly learning to read in school should first and foremost be shaped to the needs of the individual learner (Morrow, 2009; Schirmer, 2010; Wren, 2003). The International Reading Association (IRA) Board (1999) noted that teachers must be familiar with a multitude of reading instruction methods as well as have a deep understanding of how children learn in order for reading instruction to be successful.

Learning to read is not always an easy task, and one teacher—even one who is exceptional—can only do so much. This is why many literacy leaders, teachers, and administrators have come together to support their elementary, middle, and high school students by focusing on diverse reading activities before, during, and after school hours, thereby creating an educational culture that promotes and ensures effective reading practices. Guided by literacy leaders, a wide variety of materials, texts, and professional development experiences is provided to focus on instruction, motivation, reading for pleasure and information, and tools and strategies to assist those who may be at risk or simply need short-term reading assistance. These reading materials and experiences extend reading practice, improve achievement, and pique students' interest, thus setting the stage for lifelong reading (International Reading Association Board, 2000).

READERS' STRUGGLES

For the purpose of achieving a common understanding, we would like to take some time now to reflect about students and their struggles with reading. Deshler, Palinscar, Biancarosa, and Nair (2007) note that the reasons a learner may struggle with reading tasks are many and varied. Brian, a first grader, was able to read most of the words in *Horrible Harry's Secret* (Kline, 1990), but he could not understand story as a whole very well. In other words, he had exceptional decoding abilities, but he found it hard to make sense of the reading. In the same class, Anabelle spent time with *Mrs. Wishy Washy's Farm* (Crowley, 2006) and was able to determine what was happening in the story from the pictures alone and therefore able to answer a large number of comprehension questions correctly. Nonetheless, Anabelle struggled when reading the story's words, either in context or in isolation. *Both* of these first graders, one assessed to be above-average in reading ability and the other assessed to be below-average, can equally well be described as experiencing reading struggles. Some readers who struggle are unable to pronounce words and/or create meaning; which of course doesn't mean that a struggling reader can't read anything has reading difficulties all the time. It also doesn't mean that pronouncing words and creating meaning are the only areas in which struggling with reading can occur.

Some other common struggles with reading can be best elucidated by considering the characteristics of a competent reader. Proficient readers orchestrate "all their reading competencies into a fluent rendition of the text" (Moskal & Blachowicz, 2006, p. 9) that develops their own understanding of the text's meaning. Such basic reading competencies include print knowledge, prior subject knowledge, and vocabulary knowledge along with comprehension, fluency, and a toolkit of strategies to support each competency. Since, for them, reading is not difficult, proficient readers are easily engaged and motivated to read frequently for diverse purposes. Since they understand that the purposes of reading may vary, they take a different approach in reading a work of classic literature than in reading the history of the Roman Empire, and yet another in reading a math problem (Rosenblatt, 2004). Good readers can easily navigate through such recent information and communications innovations as wikis, search engines, hypertext, and other multimedia methodologies in order to accomplish research and information analysis and sharing. But, if something goes wrong within the reading process, even one considered a "good" reader may struggle.

Deshler, Palinscar, Biancarosa, and Nair (2007) suggest that many adolescent readers struggle primarily because today's accelerated reading and writing demands far exceed those experienced by past generations, and literacy instruction, especially in the area of reading comprehension, has simply not kept pace with technological change. Students are expected to read and understand a multitude of traditional literary genres along with being able to appreciate the new multimedia and Internet literacies that may involve abstruse technical data and mathematical formulas, among other things. Students nowadays must prepare themselves for a college experience or workforce demands that require high levels of reading ability and exceptional writing skills—skills often assumed as requisite even for some nonprofessional jobs in construction or manufacturing (Deshler et al., pp. 18–19).

Being a good reader involves many layers of complexity, and at any given time there can be a breakdown in any part or many parts of the learning process. Effective readers can access various strategies to assist in a fixup, and if any one strategy doesn't work for them, they immediately put others into action. Thus, struggles can emerge, however, whenever there is any serious breakdown in the learning process and the reader doesn't automatically know what to do to fix the problem.

Readers can struggle to fix a reading problem frequently or just occasionally. Those who struggle frequently may be considered at risk for failure owing to lack of sufficient preparation. For those considered at risk, each profile of reading competencies and struggles will be unique. For this reason, approaches to improvement are most effective when individual teachers work in conjunction with literacy leaders and schoolwide approaches for reading improvement. Think back to Tom, who was getting ready for seventh grade. He needed to stay focused on better understanding what he read. In the classroom, Tom learned to create images when he read. He was able to practice this strategy while reading easy books he was using to tutor a third grader in the neighborhood elementary school. He also practiced with grade-level books he was reading and while engaged in a book club sponsored by the school. When he came to feel comfortable with the strategy, he even tried it with his social studies readings while participating in a homework club. In Tom's case, the ready availability of schoolwide activities helped to focus on and therefore engage better with reading. This enhanced reading engagement, in turn, improved his reading attitude and motivation, thus spurring him to experiment with other strategies that he had learned from Mrs. Straker to improve his reading proficiency.

In increasing proficiency, assessments are key to creating a literacy profile for the school, class, and specific individuals. These literacy profiles assist literacy leaders in streamlining the curriculum and making certain that support systems and strategy instruction are in place for times when reading for meaning proves difficult. For example, a group of able readers began reading their first Alex Rider book (Horowitz, 2000) in a fourth-grade book club. Because assessments provided a literacy profile for both the class and the individuals in the book club, the teacher was sure the vocabulary would be challenging and expected that the geography might be confusing. Knowing that everyone would benefit, she made certain that instruction during the reading block focused on vocabulary and geography to enhance overall understanding. All the book club members wrote any unknown words and their looked-up meanings on post-it notes, which were organized in a notebook by book page number, and an atlas was consulted whenever the book's setting changed. With these strategies, the Alex Rider book group had little difficulty in understanding the book.

LITERACY LEADERS DESCRIBE THE STRUGGLES THAT READERS EXPERIENCE

We have surveyed both novice and experienced literacy leaders to determine what they consider to be the characteristics of a "reading struggle." In our informal sampling, we found that literacy leaders described the types of struggles readers experience in terms of eight main categories (see Table 1.1), namely, (1) letter/sound/word, (2) meaning making, (3) strategy use, (4) motivation, (5) integration/fluency, (6) practice, (7) disabilities, and (8) home environment. While this listing is just representative of our sample, it suggests the many areas that can contribute to a breakdown in reading progress for any given student. A breakdown or struggle can occur in a particular area or a combination of areas; which is why a comprehensive battery of assessments to determine students' strengths and challenges is so important and why schoolwide reading programs and activities developed by literacy leaders should be developed to support and extend learning in and beyond the classroom.

To illustrate how these various types, or facets, of reading struggles actually look in practice, let us consider a few case studies. Robert was a fourth grader whose parents spoke three different languages—Spanish, Portuguese, and English—at home, causing him some difficulty with English at school. By March in the spring term, Robert had made much progress, but he continued to struggle in many areas. His teacher determined his strengths and challenges through assessment, and a brief description of these follows, using the typology of Table 1.1.

- *Letters/sounds/words.* Robert was having difficulty in reading such multisyllable words as *admiral, charity*, and *thermometer*. He consistently struggled while reading and spelling words with -__le at the end, like *maple* and *gentle*. While reading Robert would insert words that were not printed in the text as well as substitute text words with ones that were graphically similar, like *offer* for *afford* and *whiled* for *wilted*. He was also learning the technique of reading through a word from beginning to end to ensure that he read the word actually printed in the book.

- *Meaning making.* Robert struggled more with expository text than with narrative text. He would not self-correct when his reading didn't make sense, and he would not pause to assess the meaning of an unknown word. When asked to analyze or evaluate his reading, Robert was nonresponsive. He wasn't usually sure how to answer questions geared for higher levels of thinking.

TABLE 1.1. Types of Students Reading Struggles, as Categorized by Literacy Leaders

Type of reading struggle	Description of the reading struggle
Letter/sound/word	Reading ability is compromised by a lack of strong phonological awareness, decoding skills, and/or word recognition skills.
Meaning making	Meaning is not the focus of reading, owing to issues with self-monitoring, vocabulary, background knowledge, and/or the creation of connections (to self, other texts, and the world) (Allington, 2006).
Strategy use	Readers lack sufficient action plans to implement whenever a problem occurs. They don't know, for example, practical ways to decode a multisyllable word or determine the meaning of an unknown word.
Motivation	Reading is not valued, desired, or pleasurable. Students admit that they don't like to read, have little interest in reading, or are frustrated by reading.
Integration/fluency	Problems occur owing to difficulties in orchestrating comprehension, word recognition, vocabulary, background knowledge, and motivation into a fluent rendition of the text.
Practice	Without practice, students read fewer books and are not able to improve their abilities build stamina for reading.
Disabilities	Students may have mental health, physical, learning, or behavioral disabilities that adversely affect their reading skills.
Home environment	In some homes, literacy is not supported or actively encouraged, thereby affecting the literacy learning of students.

Note. Schirmer (2010) includes linguistic (i.e., other-language) factors as an additional cause of reading struggles.

- *Strategy use.* Robert still had many strategies to add to his reading toolkit; yet, by March, for example, he was often using Question Answer Relationships (QAR; Raphael, 1986) and "read, cover, remember, retell" (Hoyt, 1999) consistently. He hadn't fully realized that you could just go back and *reread* whenever you didn't remember something! Subsequently, Robert kept a bookmark to help him remember to use these two strategies.

- *Motivation.* Robert was self-motivated in school. He wanted to do well—so, this was not an area of struggle.

- *Integration/fluency.* Robert struggled when reading expository text. He became dysfluent, had trouble with literal comprehension, and sometimes would ignore content vocabulary altogether. He forgot that he could find the meanings of new words that he encountered either posted on the classroom wall or in the book's glossary, thus making the reading much easier to understand.

Although dysfluent with expository text, Robert managed to average a reading rate of 89 correct words per minute while reading narrative text, a rate that was still below the average for his grade level. On the Multidimensional Fluency Scale (Rasinski, 2004), Robert scored as "proficient" in the areas of pace, smoothness, phrasing, and expression/volume.

• *Practice.* With both of his parents working at their self-owned restaurant, Robert wasn't sufficiently motivated to practice reading outside of school; however, he did read books about Spain at home when presented with them at school. Robert's mother was from Barcelona, and the family spent a month there the summer before the school year began.

• *Disability.* Robert did not struggle as a result of any known disability.

• *Home environment.* Robert shared time outside of school between his parent's restaurant and grandmother's apartment, which was located below his own home. He was well taken care of, but his literacy was not a high priority. Occasionally his mother would take him to the local library, but he mostly chose books with many pictures and relatively little text to read.

Robert was a struggling reader. His teacher supported him in the classroom, but she also referred him to the after-school tutoring program. This kind of schoolwide program, discussed later in this volume, not only can provide one-on-one instruction to meet the student's individual needs, but it can also enable the teacher and tutor to coordinate lessons, thereby ensuring the best possible outcome.

Turning our attention to another student, William was a sixth grader whose teacher made it clear that he was not considered a struggling reader; but he did struggle at times.

• *Letters/sounds/words.* William had acquired a solid base of sight words, could decode capably, and usually spelled unfamiliar multisyllable words correctly.

• *Making meaning.* He appeared to read for meaning with narrative texts and would ask for assistance if the assumed meaning broke down. He also appeared to read for meaning with expository text and was fluent when asked to read aloud. Benchmark assessments, however, indicated lower-than-average scores on expository text comprehension.

• *Strategy use.* William demonstrated a consistent use of strategies with narrative text but not with expository text. When reading textbooks, he did not always demonstrate strategies to retell, learn from reading, or determine the meaning of new vocabulary.

• *Motivation.* He had a neutral attitude toward academic reading and a negative attitude toward reading for pleasure. He was not motivated to read.

• *Integration/fluency.* In general, he demonstrated the ability to use a variety of strategies that allowed for the integration of reading skills.

- *Practice.* William did not believe he needed to practice reading. He did recognize that it was necessary for him to "study" his textbooks, but he didn't believe that necessarily involved his reading them from the beginning of the chapter to the end!

- *Disability.* William did not struggle as a result of any known disability.

- *Home environment.* William's dad read online and printed versions of the newspaper every day, and his mother read magazines and books. William had a bookcase overflowing with books in his room.

When asked about his reading, William explained, "My mom read all the Harry Potter books to me when I was growing up. I wanted to read the last book myself, but I never did. For Christmas she gave me the CD, but I haven't listened to it either. I will someday." In short, the problem was that William was not motivated to read. He wasn't motivated to read for either recreational or academic purposes. In fact, William rarely read anything unless he absolutely *had to* for school. So, although William could read, he didn't. This predicament is fairly common as boys enter their tween years (Sullivan, 2009), but the pattern occurs with girls too.

Those contributing to the "reading struggles" survey (see Table 1.1) definitely considered a lack of motivation as a type of reading struggle, and countless literacy leaders are disheartened that so many children and young adults consciously choose not to read for either enjoyment or to gain knowledge. To help counteract this trend, some literacy leaders have implemented book clubs before, during, or after school that foster a natural love of reading through free choice, student-selected assignments, and discussions. These book clubs are discussed at length in this book.

William read *The Hunger Games* (Collins, 2008) in a classroom-based book club. The story line and discussion with peers motivated him and many friends to read the same author's *Catching Fire* (Collins, 2009) and *Mockingjay* (Collins, 2010) for pleasure. Now, William has subscriptions to gaming and sports magazine and has started opting to read right before going to bed.

Another issue that confronted both William and Robert was successfully reading and understanding expository text. Literacy leaders find this situation to be fairly common; so they sponsor professional development sessions, discussed at length in this book, to assist teachers in selecting reading materials and implementing strategies specifically designed for expository texts.

Whatever the severity of students' reading struggles, literacy leaders have an important role to play in schools. They assist students and teachers directly, but they also implement programs and activities for students in the school that indirectly enhance classroom instruction by facilitating the acquisition of reading strategies and skills. These programs and activities are not only for those who are at risk of reading failure but also for any student who may benefit from additional reading practice.

Literacy leaders also have an important role to play in the school's community. Connecting with families to provide a focus on reading strategies and practice routines at home supports the broad acquisition and development of reading skills. Partnering with families in this way can help them see how easily they can provide additional literacy support outside of school even when their lives are so busy. This highly beneficial type of teacher–parent partnership is also described at length in this volume.

Literacy leaders play yet another important role in creating a school community of informed teachers who support reading irrespective of the specific grade they teach. This role includes the ongoing development of teachers' practices, conversations about current issues, and the implementation of innovations and technology to improve literacy learning for all students (North Central Regional Educational Library, 1996). Literacy leaders help sustain teachers' professional growth and refine their instructional methods through collaboration, experimentation, and active learning—fundamentally creating a school-based system for reading education (*Education Week,* 2004). These leaders understand theory, are able to explain it, and help their colleagues shift from theory to practice, demonstrating in the process that a theoretical framework is essential to a school culture that embraces professional development for the sake of those who are instructed. Part of this theoretical framework consists of learning theories and schools' mission statements.

ASSUMPTIONS ABOUT LEARNING: LEARNING THEORIES AND MISSION STATEMENTS

Tompkins (2010) postulates four basic reading theories that help "effective teachers understand how students learn" (p. 5). These theories, which are either teacher- or student-centered, include behaviorism, constructivism, sociolinguistics, and cognitive/information processing. Behaviorism, the only teacher-centered theory of the four, describes a situation in which the instructor teaches small, sequenced discrete reading skills in a hierarchical order. The teacher is seen as one who supplies the knowledge step by step, providing practice and review to ensure mastery through stimulus–response mechanisms (Alexander & Fox, 2004; Shepard, 2004). This theory may be considered bottom-up in that instruction, mainly focused on word recognition, moves from part to whole, starting with letters and sounds (Schirmer, 2010, p. 4).

Constructivism provides a naturalistic learning environment where the readers actively construct knowledge through purposeful and meaningful lessons. The technique is student-centered because the student, not the teacher, is at the core of the learning, and it is designated a top-down model because the readers use their own experiences and background knowledge to create their understanding. Here instruction focuses on individuals' comprehension, moving from the whole to part. In starting from the whole, readers begin by considering their life experiences and prior knowledge and then connect this information to the reading to develop meaning (Schirmer, 2010, p. 4).

Sociolinguistics stresses the importance of language and social interactions when reading and creating understanding. Both scaffolding (Bruner, 1986) and working within a zone of proximal development (Rogoff, 1990; Vygotsky, 1978) fall under the rubric of sociolinguistics. The image of a building scaffold helps to explain this concept. The more knowledgeable reader, through language and social interactions, assists a less knowledgeable reader by "scaffolding" a task, that is, building supports that better demonstrate, simplify, and explain how to proceed, striving for a positive result. With increased motivation from the assistance, the less knowledgeable reader eventually begins to demonstrate the ability to perform the task *without* assistance. At that point the scaffold is no longer needed; so, it is "dismantled" and then "rebuilt" at a point further along in the student's development where support is again considered necessary. Scaffolding ultimately enables children to accomplish tasks that they would not be able to do on their own. The zone of proximal development is, therefore, the difference between what the child can do on his or her own and what he or she can do with the scaffolding.

A final student-centered approach to readers' struggles is cognitive or information processing, which focuses on the processes that take place in the minds of both the reader and writer. Tompkins (2010) pairs cognitive processing with information processing because they are "closely aligned" (p. 11), with both viewing reading and writing as active, connected, and complex. Readers develop a personal understanding of any given text through the use of specific strategies that concentrate on meaning making and metacognition.

Implicitly reflecting these and other learning theories, mission statements explicitly reflect the school staff's beliefs about the school's educational culture. Mission statements include the school's purposes, values, and work ethic and aims (Radtke, 1998). Here is the mission statement from Diablo Vista Middle School (2010–2011) in northern California. It states the purpose ("At Diablo Vista we are here as a united community to support and encourage each other"), continues with what the educators aspire to for their students ("to become positive, well-rounded, lifelong learners and successful leaders of the future"), and concludes with the types of work in which the educators will engage:

- Provide a challenging standards-based educational program that prepares students for success in high school and beyond.
- Create an environment of educational excellence by using a variety of instructional strategies and activities to address the varied learning strengths of our students.
- Provide a caring, nurturing environment in which all students can feel supported and safe emotionally, intellectually, and physically.
- Build positive personal characteristics such as tolerance, integrity, cooperation, and honesty, and encourage respect for the individual differences that make each of us unique.

Reading curriculum and programs developed or enhanced by literacy leaders should be grounded in the school's mission statement and learning theories. At Diablo Vista teachers function as a collaborative teaching community guided by learning theory and the California state standards. Students are given opportunities to engage in the behavior of lifelong learners and successful leaders within the reading and language arts curriculum through a variety of activities, many supported by both the district's and the school's literacy leaders. A variety of research-based reading strategies are integrated across the curriculum, and supports are implemented to develop a caring, nurturing environment and confident, respectable students. Clearly the mission statement does not specifically address the problems that may arise for a reader but, rather, guides literacy leaders and teachers in developing the best possible course of action for instruction.

BALANCED READING INSTRUCTION

Examples of balanced reading instruction are found throughout this book. Tompkins's (2010) view of balanced reading instruction "is based on a comprehensive view of literacy that combines explicit instruction, guided practice, collaborative learning, and independent reading and writing" (p. 18). Balanced instruction creates successful readers largely by mixing both teacher- and student-centered methods that match learners to their respective styles of learning. It strives to employ a variety of reading strategies that in turn produce optimal learning experiences for all students. As earlier noted, no single technique or combination of techniques helps all readers achieve their goals equally well; so, a balance of techniques or methods, in general best supports individuals and groups (Morrow, 2009; Schirmer, 2010; Tompkins, 2010).

Balanced reading is systematic and uses appropriate strategies and skills to support the reading process. There is time to practice prediction, comprehension, and decoding in authentic situations (Schirmer, 2010) and to build higher-level thinking skills, with thoughtful reading selections and understanding as important components (Allington, 2006; Gunning, 2008). Allington (2006) reminds educators that students learn what they are taught, and if students are constantly engaged in balanced reading instruction and get in the habit of actually reading about 90 minutes every day, they will become competent and self-assured readers.

Some of the key components of balanced reading instruction feature recommendations suggested by the National Reading Panel (2000), which may be accessed at *www.nationalreadingpanel.org*. These are deemed "essential skills" by Bursuck and Damer (2007, p. 5), that is, necessary for those who are considered struggling, or at-risk, readers. The essential skills or components include phonemic awareness, phonics, fluency, vocabulary, and comprehension.

Additional components of balanced reading instruction cited by Tompkins (2010, p. 19) include strategy instruction for both reading and writing, thoughtful literacy applied to literature, reading and writing for both pleasure and learning purposes with a wide selection of materials and texts, and reading a variety of (electronic as well as hard copy) texts in a variety of ways (such as shared reading, guided reading, independent reading, etc.). Listening and speaking are important in balanced reading instruction, as are spelling and using the writing process. Although this volume focuses on reading, issues of writing and literacy in general are included when appropriate.

Balanced reading instruction is the goal for all readers, both those who struggle frequently and those who struggle occasionally. Literacy leaders want students of all abilities and all grade levels to be competent, thoughtful readers, and our sincere hope is that the literacy leaders, students, and families spotlighted in this book will prove inspirational and thus an additional impetus for implementing supportive practices. Those who shared their stories and insights with us did so to benefit literacy leaders and students everywhere.

CHAPTER TWO

Response to Intervention
A Framework for Supporting Diverse Readers

So please, oh PLEASE, we beg, we pray/Go throw your TV set away/
And in its place you can install/A lovely bookshelf on the wall.
—ROALD DAHL, *Charlie and the Chocolate Factory* (1964)

The art of learning to read begins with nurturing consistent support
and the pure joy in the belief in all of its potential.
—ANNEE ENGLEMANN PHILLIPS, reading teacher, Winnetka, Illinois

---

Miss Addie Perry, reading specialist at High Woods School, walks down the hall for her initial meeting with Emma in Room 1E. Emma is engaged in a classroom project when Miss Addie arrives in the classroom. The classroom teacher introduces Emma to Miss Addie, and as they are walking down the hall the following exchange takes place.

> MISS ADDIE: Hi, my name is Miss Addie. It is so nice to meet you! It is your turn to play some reading games with me today. I want to show you my special reading room in the library, and if you are ever in the library and see my light on, please come in and say "Hello."
>
> EMMA: Hi.

Miss Addie and Emma walk to the reading room while engaging in a casual conversation and building a natural sense of rapport.

> MISS ADDIE: Here we are. Let's have some fun!
>
> EMMA (*Sits at the table with Miss Addie.*)
>
> MISS ADDIE: Now we get to play some reading games. Some might be easy, and others might be a little tricky, but don't worry—I am just trying to learn about all the things you know.

And so the assessment begins ...

Allington (2008) correctly observes that "most struggling readers never catch up with their higher-achieving classmates" (p. 1). Miss Addie, the teachers, and the support staff at her school are all working to break the potential cycle of frustration and failure experienced by first graders who may initially enter school feeling insecure about their reading abilities. This damaging cycle is best avoided by making certain that the students have intensive support as they begin to learn to read. The supportive adults provide the opportunities for students to read, reread, and then read some more. Their teachers give even the slowest learners ample opportunities to catch up with their higher-achieving classmates and to feel confident of their potential to become more able readers.

Miss Addie is a veteran teacher with 15 years of experience as a regular classroom teacher and 12 years as a reading intervention specialist (RIS). High Woods School, located in a suburb of Chicago, is one of three elementary schools (kindergarten–grade 4) in the district, serving some 400 students. All schools in the district share the same philosophy of instruction, which is developmental in nature and defined by the individual needs of the children. The needs of each child change over time, thus requiring a flexible yet purposeful response from the school and its administrators.

This public school district has a long tradition of leadership in progressive public education. Throughout its history, the district has been deeply committed to the unique needs of each child, conceived holistically, and to the mastery of superior academic skills. That commitment to educational excellence is grounded in the firm belief that individualized quality education must depend upon the active involvement of both teachers and parents in the educational process.

High Woods School has achieved consistent success by adapting to each student's individual needs through a response-to-intervention (RTI) model for instruction and intervention. In discussing the role of RTI relative to the struggling reader, Miss Addie notes that the most important aspect of successfully implementing of RTI is the psychic investment one makes in the child—that is the most critical component. "Learning becomes an adventure together," Miss Addie elaborates, "as the invitation to learn about reading embraces the whole child." She believes that in a successful RTI model the support staff must expend sufficient energy from the start to make sure that the child feels completely comfortable with the process. Establishing close rapport early on in the process contributes significantly to the growth and development of a lifelong learner. An important aspect of a successful RTI framework is that it enables teachers to be problem solvers closely collaborating in a supportive process intended to develop each individual child's potential.

RTI strategies are used in both academic and behavioral programs. In this chapter, after examining the goals and methods of RTI in general, we focus on strategies utilized to implement RTI in the area of reading and writing.

BACKGROUND OF RTI

Response to intervention is a comprehensive early detection and prevention approach that identifies struggling students and assists them in classrooms before they fall behind. The original RTI initiative was outlined in the U.S. Congress 2004 reauthorization of the Individuals with Disabilities Education Act (IDEA). Briefly, the purpose of RTI is to provide struggling readers with expert intervening instruction so that they will not need special education services and/or placements. Although RTI was originally conceived as a means of early identification and determination of special education eligibility, it is increasingly becoming a significant overall framework for school improvement through general education.

RTI promotes all students' achievement by closely monitoring their responses to instruction and adjusting that instruction based on their progress (Bocala, Mello, Reedy, & Lacireno-Paquet, 2009). RTI is not an inflexible model to be imposed on schools, but rather a framework to help schools identify and support students before literacy difficulties interfere with their learning and become truly serious. As Allington (2008) enthused, referring to RTI, "I've called it perhaps our last, best hope" (p. 20). Barnes and Harlacher (2008) offer this definition: "RTI is a multi-tiered method of service delivery in which all students are provided an appropriate level of evidence-based instruction" (p. 417). The hallmarks of exemplary RTI programs are universal screening and high-quality instruction for all students, with a special focus on interventions targeted for struggling students.

In RTI models, there are some elements that are consistent and some that vary from school to school. These elements are common to all RTI implementations: following sequential steps for identifying students who need help at the beginning of and throughout the school year; utilizing scientifically based interventions; collecting data over time for all students who struggle; and using data for instructional decision making. Decisions in the RTI framework are always based on students' performance data, not someone's opinion.

In this chapter, we discuss five major considerations that must be dealt with when fully implementing RTI in elementary schools, namely:

1. School leadership and fostering a community of learners
2. Universal screening and initial diagnostic assessment
3. Progress monitoring
4. Curriculum and instruction across three tiers
5. Engaging parents in partnerships

In the lower elementary grades, students experiencing reading difficulties need their teachers to intervene to prevent future reading failure. We offer specific recommendations in this chapter to help educators identify those students nost in need of help and, equally importantly, to implement research-based interventions aimed at assuring that everyone succeeds in reading well. Appendix 2.1, at the end of the chapter, lists several websites that offer additional information on RTI.

SCHOOL LEADERSHIP AND FOSTERING A COMMUNITY OF LEARNERS

Leadership to Support a Positive School Climate and Culture

To assure both effective implementation and the long-term sustainability of the RTI model, strong and collaborative administrative leadership from the top is imperative. To monitor the significant changes that need to occur when implementing RTI initiatives, the school's teachers and support staff need to work closely together. Constant and consistent dialogue among school staff members and administrators is essential to make certain that all students receive the early interventions they need to develop as secure readers and writers. To move the RTI model from pure theory to actual practice, all staff members must create sufficient time for the internal dialogue, problem-solving meetings, and the development of action plans that will enable the RTI model to succeed.

Educators Saphier and King (1985) have identified a number of cultural norms that are conducive to a positive school climate, including collegiality, a willingness to experiment, high expectations, trust and caring, a sense of celebration and humor, wide-based involvement in decision making, a tendency to protect what's important, a sense of tradition, and honest and open communications. Barth's (2002) assessment was that, "these qualities dramatically affect the capacity of a school to improve—and to promote learning" (p. 7).

Besides seeking to cultivate cultural norms as these, principals also ideally exhibit the following characteristics: they demonstrate instructional leadership, support professional development, foster a collaborative climate, focus on student achievement, and understand the change process.

The Principal's and Teachers' Role as Interventionists

The principal's role is crucial in setting expectations for the successful implementation of the RTI model, but equally critical to success is the willingness of teachers to implement the interventions faithfully and effectively. General education teachers may not always see themselves as "interventionists" and indeed may even resist the expectation that they should provide individualized interventions as a routine part of their classroom practice (Walker, Ramsey, & Gresham, 2004). It is the principal who must help teachers move toward a better understanding of their new role as interventionists.

Implementation of RTI must combine the knowledge and willingness to change for the better with sufficient provision to examine the curriculum of the school. A principal who values consensus building and collaboration among faculty and support staff helps assure the success of all RTI initiatives undertaken. The school's chief leader must believe that correctly assessing students' instructional needs is the underlying rationale for RTI. In furthering its aims, the school principal also needs to:

- Initiate the specific measures and work to provide appropriate resources for instruction.
- Find ways to integrate the most productive assessment techniques with ongoing plans and programs.
- Convey the conviction that teachers and administrators are a unified team in which all students are honored.
- Involve him- or herself wholeheartedly in the problem-solving process.
- Be an invested and supportive member of the team, monitoring each child personally as the process unfolds.
- Aid the working groups in their decision making, collaborating effectively to produce better overall results.
- Actively foster the growth of teachers as learners and leaders.

Fostering a Community of Learners

Another important characteristic of schools able to develop successful RTI programs is the school staff's commitment to developing a community of learners. Such a "community of learners" is a key attribute of any educational environment, whether in the individual classroom or a school (Peterson, 1992).

At High Woods School, there is a strong tradition of developing a community of learners. The school district's website proclaims: "With a tradition of leadership in progressive public education, the [district] Public Schools consider each child to be a whole person who should be developed intellectually, socially, emotionally and physically." The district's defining document, "A Community of Learners," declares "the schools' primary purpose to be the development of each child's ability to read with comprehension, write and speak effectively, perform mathematical processes with precision, use the scientific method, and act with confidence and self-reliance." Schools seeking to successfully implement the RTI model must create a community of learners that values both the affective and cognitive development of each child.

Implementating Recommendations for Leadership and Community Building

Roland Barth, a former teacher, principal, and member of the faculty of Harvard University (where he founded the Harvard Principals' Center and the International Network of Principals), has written extensively on the importance of a collegial culture in schools to promote learning. He states, "The vision is, first, that the school will be a community, a place full of adults and students who care" (Barth, 2002, p. 11). At High Woods School, Miss Addie recommends the following steps for making the RTI model a priority in the school and for moving from a purely philosophical understanding of the model to imple-mentating specific interventions:

- Creating a task force or team of faculty members who volunteer to brainstorm about RTI and problem-solve about the delivery of services.
- Asking faculty members to bring proposals and their own observations and sug-gestions to the task force and to organize a small volunteer group to study poten-tial RTI.
- Allowing time for these faculty members to present their findings on RTI and working diligently with them to develop a deeper understanding of the system.

UNIVERSAL SCREENING AND INITIAL DIAGNOSTIC ASSESSMENT

Universal screening is a step taken by school personnel early in the school year to deter-mine which students are at risk for not meeting grade-level standards. It can be accom-plished by either reviewing the recent results of state tests or by administering academic or behavioral screening assessments to the students at any given grade level, and those students whose scores fall below a certain cutoff point are identified as needing more specialized academic or behavioral interventions. This initial process of assessment is a critical component of the RTI model, one that High Woods School enacts scrupulously to assure that all its students receive the services needed to succeed.

Close collaboration by school staff members in developing, implementating, and monitoring the intervention process also characterizes the beginning of every school year at High Woods School. Screening assessments are quick and efficient tools that are highly accurate predictors of student performance.

Diagnostic screening is key to helping to plan effective instruction and intervention because a major focus of the RTI model is using data to drive critical instructional deci-sion making about those students who must need help. To support a flexible but reliable approach to RTI, sufficient ongoing information must be constantly available to identify the academic and behavioral needs of individual students. This is necessary to design and alter instructional plans to meet the needs of all students especially struggling learn-ers as they develop over time.

Time-Line of Universal Screening Assessments (Based on High Woods School)

Fall—Kindergarten

Kindergarten at High Woods School is play-based. Informal screening may involve stu-dents whom teachers observe struggling with reading at the beginning of the school year. Some students, based on teachers' discretion, are screened by means of a teacher-devised game called the Lollipop Test; which provides information about alphabetic knowledge and sight–sound connections with alphabet recognition. Universal screening typically does not begin until the winter months, or second half, of kindergarten.

Winter—Kindergarten

During the second half of kindergarten, all the students are screened by using the Lollipop Test, based on alphabet recognition and closely related to the Illinois Snapshots of Early Literacy (ISEL; Barr, Blachowicz, & Buhle, 2004). The ISEL is also used at teachers' discretion to assess the core skills of young children. Specific ISEL components assess phonemic awareness (the ability to identify and manipulate sounds), alphabetic knowledge (the awareness of individual letters and letter names), the concept of *word* (i.e., the ability to segment spoken sentences or phrases into words), phoneme correspondence (the ability to identify the correspondence between letters and sounds), and sight word knowledge (a list of common words). It is important to note that any screening instrument that does not comprehensively cover all the core skills may be ineffective in identifying those children who display limitations in only a particular area of early literacy (Justice, Invernizzi, & Meier, 2002).

Fall—First Grade

All first graders at High Woods are assessed with the ISEL, which generally consists of sets of standardized, individually administered measures of early literacy development for grades K–2. Each grade's edition consists of brief measures of performance that can be used regularly to monitor the development of early literacy skills. The Illinois Snapshots of Early Literacy for Grade 2 (ISEL-2), for example, assesses the essential literacy skills that students need for success in reading.

The Illinois Snapshots of Early Literacy—Kindergarten/First Grade (ISEL-K/1; Barr et al., 2004) was designed as a classroom-based assessment for the use of kindergarten and first-grade teachers, having as its aims:

- To help identify the literacy needs of their students.
- To guide in the design of meaningful instructional lessons.
- To identify students who may need access to an early reading intervention tutorial program.
- To enable students to meet the Illinois Learning Standards.

An important aspect of first-grade testing is that the students are not pulled out of the classroom for screening during the first 3 weeks of school in order for the classroom teachers to work on developing a strong community of learners. Instead, first graders are screened as the first month of school ends. Classroom teachers in the first grade also fill out observation forms detailing students' reading behaviors and use of strategies.

Fall—Second through Fourth Grades

High Woods School uses AIMSweb (Hampton-Brown, 2010) for initial screening in the first through fourth grades. AIMSweb is a benchmark and progress monitoring system based on direct, frequent, and continuous student assessment. The results, reported to students, parents, teachers, and administrators through a web-based data management and reporting system, help assess the progress of RTI programs through three key measures:

1. *Benchmark*, which assesses all students three times per year for universal screening (early identification), general and special education progress monitoring, and adequate yearly progress (AYP) accountability.
2. *Strategic monitor*, which monitors at-risk students monthly and evaluates the effectiveness of instructional changes.
3. *Progress monitor*, which consists of written individualized annual goals and more frequent monitoring for those in need of more intensive instructional services.

Data Analysis: Grades K–4

Once the data are gathered, the next step involves having all the classroom teachers and support staff (e.g., the reading specialist, speech teacher, special education teacher, social worker, school psychologist, and principal) get together and analyze the data. At High Woods School this task entails a half-day release day for teachers three times a year. Each child is reviewed individually to determine what specific help is needed. The process entails an especially close appraisal of those students who struggle with reading tasks the most. Each child is discussed and data, including any individualized education program (IEP) information, are shared with teachers and support staff.

Recommendations for Structuring and Organizing Universal Screening

The research on reading intervention is unequivocal in stating that early identification and timely interventions are critical in preventing or minimizing reading problems (Snow, Burns, & Griffin, 1998). Effective tools need to be mobilized within an RTI framework so that school staff members fully understand the purposes, advantages, and limitations of the specific universal screening methods employed in their school. To properly structure and organize universal screening for students in a school, the following instructions should be observed:

- Develop user-friendly forms for the support staff and faculty.
- Structure time during school for half-day meetings to review each child individu-

ally and to decide jointly which students warrant intervention—and the specific type of intervention.

- Design recommended time lines that help track students' progress for the faculty's input.
- Make they key decisions only after sufficient data are collected, and ensure that there is a record of what needs to be done and the subsequent outcomes.
- Decide jointly (i.e., the faculty with the support staff) who will carry out each intervention and how that person will be supported for each student needing help.
- Schedule consistent meeting times and locations for ongoing progress monitoring.
- Permit teacher using the ISEL-K/1 as a pre- and postassessment tool for accurately documenting students' growth in literacy to also use additional classroom and district literacy assessments for supplementary help in documentation.

PROGRESS MONITORING

In the RTI model, progress monitoring entails a set of assessment procedures for determining the extent to which students are benefiting from classroom instruction and for monitoring the effectiveness of the curriculum. To be effective, progress monitoring measures must be available in several forms that are comparable in difficulty and conceptualization and yet representative of the performance desired at the end of the year (Fuchs, Compton, Fuchs, & Bryant, 2008). At High Woods School, students are first assessed for progress some 6–8 weeks after their initial screening.

Progress monitoring assessments are brief probes that provide teachers with ongoing information about students' responses to interventions. The goal of these assessments is to provide teachers with the requisite data to answer two questions conclusively, namely:

1. Is the student making progress toward the grade-level expectation or long-term goal?
2. Is the student making progress toward mastery of the targeted skill?

It is important during the progress monitoring process that assessors check not only students' level of performance but also their rate of learning. Teachers must be trained to use these assessments effectively to quantify rates of progress and subsequently adjust the educational program for struggling students (Fuchs, Fuchs, & Zumeta, 2008). Without sufficient teacher training, the usefulness of any progress monitoring measure may be greatly limited. High Woods School supports data-driven approaches and continues to work with faculty to help classroom teachers with the critical progress monitoring phase of RTI. When progress monitoring is implemented correctly, its benefits include:

- Accelerated learning, because students are receiving more appropriate instruction.
- More informed instructional decisions.
- Documentation of students' progress for accountability purposes.
- More efficient communication with families and other professionals about the students' progress.
- Higher expectations for the students by teachers.
- Fewer special education referrals. (Habrouch, Woldbeck, Ihnot, & Parker, 1999; *www.studentprogress.org*)

In conclusion, progress monitoring assessments need to measure the essential skills that children are learning to develop as strong readers and writers. These assessments are given over time to document not only students' level of performance but also their rate of learning. In High Woods School, generally these assessments are undertaken every 6–8 weeks. However, how often the measures are made depends on not only the skill(s) being assessed but also each individual child's prior progress.

Recommendations for Progress Monitoring

The main factor determining the frequency of progress monitoring is the specific goal for each child's literacy development and the particular intervention. Progress monitoring might well be weekly or it might be every 8 weeks. Classroom teachers and support staff should work together to schedule reliable times to meet and discuss the students to assess their reading progress and skill development. Response to intervention is an increasingly popular educational approach to instruction, assessment, and intervention designed to provide effective data-based interventions for struggling students. Although RTI was conceived as a means of early identification and determination of special education eligibility, it is fast becoming the preferred overall approach to school improvement through general education. RTI, then, has become a comprehensive support system to promote the achievement of all students by first monitoring their responses to instruction and then adjusting subsequent instruction based on the students' progress (Bocala et al., 2009).

CURRICULUM AND INSTRUCTION ACROSS THREE TIERS

The RTI model is normally a three-tiered system of interventions designed to meet the needs of *all* students collectively. Curriculum based on state-mandated standards and high-quality instruction are essential components for students' achieving success. Tier 1 instruction is generally defined as reading instruction provided to *all* the students in a given class. Beyond this general definition, there is no clear consensus on the meaning of the term *Tier 1*. Tier 1 instruction includes high-quality research-based curricula and instructional strategies that support the district's curriculum guidelines. Tier 1 provides core instruction and flexible grouping that targets specific skills so that the instructional goals for all students can be met.

Tier 2 interventions are provided only to students who have difficulty with screening measures or weak progress in regular classroom instruction. Tier 2 students receive, in addition to general classroom instruction, supplemental small-group reading instruction aimed at building foundational reading skills. That is, Tier 2 offers supplemental instruction in addition to the standards-based curriculum received in Tier 1. The curriculum and instruction in Tier 2 are designed to meet the needs of students not progressing upto expectations in Tier 1 activities.

Tier 3 interventions are provided to students who do not progress after a reasonable amount of time spent with Tier 2 interventions and therefore require more intensive assistance. Tier 3 (or, in districts with more than three tiers, Tiers 3 and above) usually entails one-on-one tutoring, with a mix of instructional interventions. Tier 3 instruction also includes more explicit instruction that is normally focused on a specific skill need, whether an accelerated or remedial need. Close ongoing analysis of student performance is critical to success in Tier 3 interventions. Systematically collected data are used to identify the successes and failures in instruction for individual students in this tier. If students still experience difficulty after receiving intensive Tier 3 services, they are evaluated for possible inclusion in special education programs. The following questions are addressed to make concrete decisions about special education services.

- *Problem identification*—What Is the Problem? Is It Significant?
- *Problem analysis*—Why Is the Problem Occurring?
- *Plan development*—What Are We Going to Do about It?
- *Plan evaluation*—Did the Plan Work?

The ongoing analysis of students' performance is a critical daily function at High Woods School. Faculty and support staffs members cooperate to ensure the best delivery of services for each child. Assessment data are reviewed systematically over time to determine each student's progress and to inform his or her parents accordingly. Students still experiencing reading difficulties are discussed at length during regular problem-solving team meetings that include the classroom teacher, the reading specialist, and any other staff members needed to help refine the particular intervention plan. If greater attention is needed, a multidisciplinary committee (MDC) meeting may be scheduled. A typical MDC includes the classroom teacher, the reading specialist, the learning disability specialist, the psychologist, and the principal, and together they determine whether or not to recommend an evaluation of the student by the special education team.

Using Reading Recovery as an Intervention

At High Woods School, Miss Addie utilizes the Reading Recovery model as an intervention for students struggling with reading. Clay (1987), who developed Reading Recovery, advanced the argument that many struggling readers are in fact "instructionally disabled" because they have never received appropriate or sufficient instructional opportunities. Vellutino, Fletcher, Snowling, and Scanlon (2004) also cited research that focused on the lack of instructional opportunities as well, noting that "many poor readers are impaired because of inadequate instruction or other experiential factors" (p. 2). The RTI initiative is intended to provide high-quality instructional opportunities for struggling readers to minimize this problem, and Ms. Addie believed that employing the Reading Recovery model in the first-grade intervention plan would definitely benefit struggling readers during their early literacy development and help to remedy or prevent reading problems in subsequent grades.

ENGAGING PARENTS IN PARTNERSHIPS

When families, schools, and communities work together closely, children are more successful in school and schools improve. High Woods School has created effective partnerships that include parents, families, students, community members, and educators. Ms. Addie notes that indicators of an effective partnership include sharing information, problem solving, and celebrating student success. Central to effective partnerships is the shared responsibility and shared ownership of students' challenges and successes.

When forming partnerships, one must constantly seek to nurture the collaborative process. To develop true collaboration, parents and guardians must be fundamentally involved in the entire educational experience. Parents should be recognized as having important information and expertise that can contribute significantly to the partnership. School personnel should provide parents with all relevant information and empower them to be equal partners in supporting their child's learning. At Tier 1, parental involvement in school decision making leads to an improved positive school climate. Parents and guardians are seen as key partners in all aspects of RTI, but their role may shift at each tier of intervention. In particular, at the targeted (Tier 2) and intensive (Tier 3) levels, their expertise in knowing about and dealing with their own child becomes vital. At these tiers, members of the student's family may well provide key information about him or her that suggests strategies leading to much-improved outcomes.

Collaboration is more than simply working together and more than just linkage; it is agreeing to formally come together to achieve mutually desired outcomes. If one is to believe the adage "It takes a village to raise a child," then the wider community always has a vested interest in supporting a positive school climate, which research consistently concludes leads to better academic results. Furthermore, school officials should recognize that cultural understanding requires more than simple awareness. Understanding and respect for cultural differences become vital ingredients when attempting to engage families and foster community support for favorable learning outcomes.

At High Woods School, the successful implementation of RTI requires that parents interact actively with the school community. Parents become involved in all levels of the discussions that pertain to their child's participation in RTI programs. Parents are notified immediately and early in the process regarding their child's initial screening, diagnosis, and participation in all interventions.

BENEFITS OF THE RTI MODEL

Perhaps the greatest benefit of the RTI model is that it prevents a "wait-to-fail" situation from developing because students get help promptly. In High Woods School, as soon as assessment data indicate a problem area for a student, interventions are put into place to address these concerns. Classroom teachers and support staff work hand in hand to develop the best instructional program for each individual child. By enabling the team of specialists and classroom teachers to intervene early and interface with the student daily, correctly implemented RTI procedures directly address the needs of the struggling reader. RTI approaches also specify that if a child proves nonresponsive to various interventions, further investigation occurs. A lack of response to attempted interventions may suggest that a disability is responsible that could require special education programs and services. The RTI model helps "close the gap between identification and treatment." The RTI emphasis is on "treatment validity" (Fuchs & Fuchs, 1998, p. 204), thus moving the identification process away from diagnosing deficits to examining student outcomes—and thereby enables the Emmas, by the end of first grade, to be well on their way to becoming successful (hopefully, lifelong) readers and writers.

IMPLEMENTING KEY IDEAS

Response to intervention is a comprehensive early detection and prevention approach that identifies struggling readers and immediately assists them in the classroom before they fall far behind. Despite its overall positive impact, RTI often poses challenges to school districts in being successfully implemented. This chapter has reviewed five major considerations in successfully implementing this approach in schools to support the academic progress of both readers and writers:

- Strong school leadership and fostering a community of learners.
- Clear guidelines for universal screening and initial diagnostic assessments.
- Appropriate progress monitoring to assure suitable rates of learning.
- High quality curriculum instruction across three tiers to meet the needs of *all* students.
- Effective methods to engage parents in partnerships.

CONCLUDING THOUGHTS

The RTI model puts all the focus on a child's needs in a collaborative process in the schoolhouse that promotes learning for everyone. At High Woods School, Miss Addie believes that the procedure enables teachers to be problem solvers in a supportive process, with the focus on the development of each individual child. Everyone is responsible for all the children.

APPENDIX 2.1. USEFUL INTERNET SITES FOR RTI

www.ilispa.org

The Illinois School Psychologists Association (ISPA) is a not-for-profit professional association that has represented school psychologists in Illinois since 1979.

www.scoe.org

The Sonoma County Office of Education (SCOE) website provides a collection of reading and language arts resources and information designed to support teachers, administrators, parents, and anyone else concerned with improving literacy in Sonoma County and beyond. Formerly known as the Reading Corner, the website has its web pages compiled by Dr. Kevin Feldman, SCOE's reading and early intervention consultant.

www.interventioncentral.org

This website provides teachers, schools, and districts with free articles and tools to successfully implement RTI. The site was created by Jim Wright, an RTI consultant and trainer from central New York who has worked for 17 years in public schools as a school psychologist and administrator.

www.nwrel.org/nwrcc/nclb/RtI.php

This website of the Northwest Regional Education Laboratory (NWREL), a nationwide network of centers created by the U.S. Department of Education, provides assistance to states regarding the Elementary and Secondary Education Act (ESEA) and other educational reforms, including RTI.

www.RtINetwork.org

This website is dedicated to the effective implementation of RTI in school districts nationwide. Its goal is to guide educators and families in the large-scale implementation of RTI so that each child has access to high-quality instruction and so that struggling students and those with learning disabilities are identified and receive the support needed to be successful.

iris.peabody.vanderbilt.edu/RtI01_overview/chalcycle.htm

Ideas and Research for Inclusive Settings (IRIS) is a website dedicated to providing high-quality resources for college and university faculty and professional development providers about students with disabilities. IRIS seeks to attain this goal by providing free online interactive training enhancements that translate research about the education of students with disabilities into practice.

www.RtI4success.org

This website of the American Institutes for Research and researchers from Vanderbilt University and the University of Kansas, through funding from the U.S. Department of Education's Office of Special Education Programs (OSEP), provides technical assistance to states and districts and builds the capacity of states to assist districts in implementing proven models for RTI/early intervention services.

state.RtI4success.org

This website provides resources on a number of topics related to RTI. The resources, which range from policy documents and briefs to specialized training and tools, were developed by states, districts, or territories in the United States engaged in different stages of implementing RTI.

www.aimsweb.com

This website is dedicated to developing a comprehensive benchmark and progress monitoring system based on direct, frequent, and continuous student assessment. The results are reported to students, parents, teachers, and administrators via a web-based data management and reporting system that recommends appropriate RTI initiatives.

CHAPTER THREE

Reading Interventions

What a child can do today with assistance, she will be able
to do by herself tomorrow.
—LEV VYGOTSKY

- -

On one unseasonably cold morning in Santa Clara, California, reading specialists are
beginning their rounds. Each highly qualified with a master of reading degree, Reading
Recovery certifications, or both, these specialists work together with classroom teachers across the entire district to support the first- and second-grade students whose initial and ongoing reading assessments show that they are not yet proficient. As part of
the reading intervention specialist (RIS) program, these literacy leaders provide reading
strategy practice to supplement that of the classroom teacher, using the same structure for record keeping, planning, implementation, and assessment across all the district
schools. Julie collaborated with district literacy leaders and administrators to develop the
RIS program, and she continues to be involved with the program's implementation and
evaluation.

- -

This chapter includes descriptions of two intervention programs of students at risk
for reading failure. One, the RIS program, is implemented throughout a school district,
while the other, the Literacy Learning Clinic, is implemented after school at one elementary school. Suggestions for developing other intervention programs and resources are
offered. A typical morning spent with Julie provides a better understanding of the organization and implementation of the RIS program.

THE RIS PROGRAM IN ACTION

Julie wheels her cart into room 15 of Pomeroy School. The room is warm despite the cold
weather, and there is a quiet hum while the second graders busily go about their literacy

tasks. Several students are reading, others are writing, and six are seated at a horseshoe-shaped table for guided reading with their teacher. Every child is on task.

Julie steps to a small circular table and removes a thick folder of lesson plans and record sheets, four composition notebooks, four books, magnetic letters, and a whiteboard from her cart. While she is unpacking, four students leave their desks, toting plastic bags of books from previous reading sessions, and join Julie. Without a word, each student takes a composition notebook and begins reading.

This notebook, called a Word Book, is used to teach high-frequency words. On a right-hand page, a high-frequency word is written at the top of the page first by Julie and then five times below by the student. On the back, a sentence using the word is dictated by the child to Julie. Below the sentence the word's meaning is embedded in the sentence and rendered in a drawing. The sentence and picture enable the students to use meaning, structure, and visual sources to read the high-frequency words in isolation. See Figure 3.1 for examples from a student's Word Book.

To practice for automaticity, each day the four students read the words and sentences at their own pace. If they are unsure of a word, they turn the page, read the sentence, and then return to the word on the front page. Usually they remember the word after reading the sentence and viewing the picture, because this page includes the meaning, syntax, and visual cues that provide the scaffold they need.

On this particular day, the students eventually come to a right-hand page where there is only one word. It is a high-frequency word that Julie introduced the day before. They read the single word and point to each letter as they spell it aloud. They take an

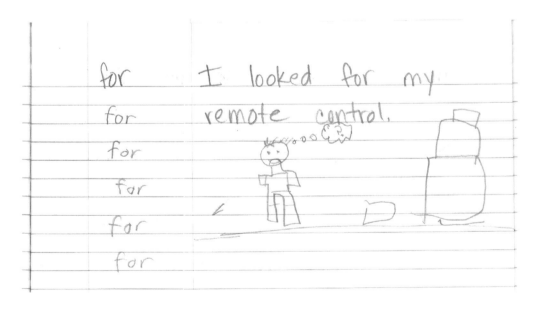

FIGURE 3.1. Examples from a student's Word Book.

index card, cover the word, and write it below, announcing each letter as they write the word five times in all, covering the prior words with the index card as they go along.

High-frequency words are introduced in the Word Book only once or twice a week. After writing the new word five times, the students individually dictate a sentence using the word, Julie writes the sentence, the student reads it back and then draws a picture that illustrates the sentence.

As the drawings are completed, each student retrieves a book from the individual book bags and begins to read aloud the selection the group read the day before. Julie records a running record of one student's reading, but listens to the others as well. Julie leans over to assist one of the boys with a word recognition strategy he is practicing before returning to her running record. As the students finish, they place the book from which they were reading aloud back in their bag.

Julie shows them the cover of the new book they are going to read. She tells them a bit about the story, using the vocabulary that is found in the book. "He can be a naughty dog," Julie says, and then asks, "What might a naughty dog do?" Since the students' answers show that they know the meaning of *naughty*, Julie tells them the names of the characters and then inquires, "What can you do if you are reading, and you read a word, but it doesn't make sense?"

"Sound out the first two or three letters, and reread it to see if you are right," answers one student.

"And," says another, "you need to be sure it makes sense."

The new book is opened and handed to the first child, who is asked to find the word *where* on page 3. The student points to *where*, flips to the beginning, and begins reading aloud. About a minute later, Julie gives the same title to the next child, repeating the procedure until all four students have their books and are reading. Julie listens carefully so she can (1) assist when needed, (2) record anecdotal observations for each student, and (3) determine which reading strategies are being implemented.

Kelly, one of the girls, reads "The dog is bagging for food" and continues to read.

"Wait," Julie says to her, "that doesn't make sense."

Knowing which word to review, Kelly begins sounding out the word, sliding along the letters with her finger as she attempts it: "be ... being ... begging! The dog is begging for food." Julie smiles to confirm that she is right, makes a quick notation in her anecdotal records, and continues to listen until all are finished. But before moving to the next activity, Julie reviews the strategies to use when the reading doesn't make sense, repeating the same strategies shared as the reading began, demonstrates how Kelly used the strategy, and then implements a comprehension exercise.

The magnetic letters and whiteboard are passed out, and Julie waits for the children's complete attention as she creates the word see in the middle of the whiteboard. "*See!*" the students chime in together. Again, making sure they are all watching, Julie sets up the whiteboard as shown in Figure 3.2. Julie asks individuals, taking turns, to manipulate the letters and make such words as tree, bee, sleep, and beep. The students then drag their fingers under the letters as they pronounce them to make sure the sounds

b		m
tr	see	p
sl		d
str		t

FIGURE 3.2. Whiteboard set up to make words with movable magnetic letters.

and letters match. Kelly creates the word *beep* but reads it as *bip*. Then she immediately recognizes the problem and corrects herself.

When 30 minutes have elapsed, it's time for Julie to move on to the next group in a different classroom. The children return to their desks as Julie neatly returns the materials to her cart and nods a farewell to the classroom teacher, who is almost ready to meet with the same four students in another guided reading session.

A Look at the Lesson's Structure

Similarly structured lessons are repeated with some 500 targeted at-risk first and second graders in all 17 schools in the district. Everything the literacy leaders do in their teaching emphasizes strategic reading that encourages and enables students to become self-sufficient. Moreover, the lesson itself unfolds in much the same way each time so that students come to have a clear understanding not only of the lesson's structure but also of how the lesson's components work together to reinforce good reading habits.

The prototypical RIS lesson consists of four research-based elements (Clay, 1991; Dorn, French, & Jones, 1998; Morris, 2005; Pressley, 2002; Schirmer, 2010): (1) Word Book activities, (2) the reading of familiar text with running record assessments (Clay, 2006), (3) the reading of unfamiliar text accompanied by anecdotal recordings, and (4) word work (activities to support word reading) activities. These four elements come together differently for each group of children since the needs of each student are unique. In other words, lesson plans are developed daily based on the unique strengths and challenges of the students in the group on any given day. Julie worked with five different groups that December morning, and although the four components were the same, the lessons reflected what the students in each group needed to practice. For example, during the word work component, one group worked on isolating letter sounds, another on separating onset and rime, and others worked on creating new words by using analogies.

As the 30-minute lesson begins, Julie pays close attention to students' automaticity in word reading. As the four students read the familiar text, Julie closely assesses a different student's reading each session with a running record to document students' strategic reading behaviors but still pays attention to the rest of the readers in case she needs to supply a reading prompt. After the new reading selection and vocabulary are introduced, a single particular reading strategy is highlighted, and a word search is performed. The four students then read the new selection aloud in turn, and Julie pays close attention to each one, pointing out miscues as they occur and recommending useful strategies. She listens carefully, supplying background support and verbal prompts whenever the reader gets stuck on a particular word. After a comprehension activity, word work is an interactive way to link decoding and encoding strategies with reading text.

Throughout the lesson, Julie takes extensive notes on the blank portion of her lesson plan intended for written notes, anecdotal observations, and running records. Armed with this information, Julie is able to encapsulate a great deal of formal and informal assessment data that will assist her in planning future lessons, deciding upon appropriate strategies, and determining who will be ready to "graduate" from the RIS program.

Positive Results

The data collected from the first 2 years of the RIS program at the Santa Clara Unified School District showed that by the end of second grade there was no longer as large a reading gap between students involved in the RIS program and the rest of their grade-level peers. For example, while the average gap in text levels between first-grade RIS and non-RIS students in the fall was 3.0, by the spring the average text-level gap had decreased to 2.5. Similarly, the average gap in text levels between second-grade RIS and non-RIS students in the fall was 2.6, but by the spring it had been reduced to 0.55. Clearly, the initial data present evidence of a strong program, but the impact of the RIS specialists extends even beyond the children taught.

Mary Kay Going, the district's director of curriculum and instruction, notes that the RIS program was developed with a strong focus on early reading intervention, but that focus extends to active collaboration from the participating classroom teachers. RIS specialists work closely with classroom teachers through team work and professional development sessions on the reading process. The professional development sessions are so well received that classroom teachers attend year after year, thereby continuing to increase their knowledge.

Another key component of the RIS program is that the RIS specialists themselves meet together frequently as a team to learn and grow, mostly discussing reading assessment, theory, and strategies. They are strongly committed to their own professional development as well as to demonstrating the efficacy of the RIS program model to other districts and schools. This dedicated corps of specialists helps to assure the reading success of every child across the district. This intervention program has become so popular among teachers throughout the district that kindergarten, third grade, and special education have been added to the program. Whatever its prospects for continued future growth, this exemplary teaching method serves its useful ends daily.

The reading specialists in the Santa Clara Unified School District are dedicated to improving the reading abilities of students. Morris (2005) stresses how important it is to assist readers who struggle in first and second grades because successful early readers are more likely to learn during their entire school careers and therefore less likely to drop out. Successful early readers are also more likely to become successful adult readers who make positive contributions to their families and communities.

AN INTERVENTION PROGRAM PARTNERING READING SPECIALIST CANDIDATES AND AT-RISK READERS

Morris (2005) believes that many models can provide the assistance needed to meet the needs of struggling readers. The RIS program was initially developed for first and second graders, but there are also intervention programs for at-risk upper elementary, middle, and high school readers. The Literacy Learning Clinic is one model of a one-on-one tutoring intervention program that supports those considered to be most at risk for reading failure at any given elementary school.

The Literacy Learning Clinic pairs at-risk readers from a kindergarten through fifth grade school with teachers who are reading specialist candidates at Saint Mary's College of California. Saint Mary's College is a private LaSallian college with a tradition of service and quality education for underrepresented populations. The Saint Mary's reading specialist candidates practice their craft at a school where many of the students' families speak a language other than English, cannot afford private tutoring, and in many cases cannot assist their children with school work. Since 2001 an average of some 24 readers annually, readers who were considered the most at risk for failure, spent productive time in the Literacy Learning Clinic, resulting in accelerated achievement, improved motivation, and life-changing experiences for many of them.

The after-school program provides a full battery of pre- and postassessments, with a unique instructional plan for each at-risk child invited to participate as well as weekly communication with classroom teachers, parents, and guardians. In addition, the school principal often visits the clinic, keeping up to date on students' progress. Because so many stakeholders are involved, students benefit from their own improved attendance, higher self-esteem, and a better understanding of reading.

The Partnership

Mary, a reading specialist and consultant from the school district, was a graduate of Saint Mary's College Reading Masters Program. She coordinates the intervention program at the school by meeting with teachers to discuss potential students, making the initial contact with parents and guardians (both by phone and in person), and supervising the reading candidates. This close supervision enables her to see the at-risk students' learning process in action firsthand. The knowledge she accumulates thereby is invaluable in better enabling her to scaffold teaching for the reading specialist candidates; also, the social, behavioral, and academic information she gleans about the students typically surpasses that of a teacher embedded in a classroom setting of 30 or more children.

Mary explained:

"The classroom teachers seek out St. Mary's Clinic for their students because they witness the students' learning transferring in their classrooms. The two-way flow of information about the students benefits everyone. Parents ask to have their child in the clinic because of success stories they have heard from other families. Most importantly, the students themselves experience success with reading and writing. They see themselves as successful learners for the first time in their school career. It is definitely a life-changing experience for all the participants."

Mary partners with the reading and language arts program director at Saint Mary's College, who is responsible for the overall organization of the clinic itself and who for the past few years has both supervised the clinic's coursework and taught certain seminars. Reading specialist candidates begin by learning how to assess students' reading abilities, match that assessment to instruction, and plan and implement lessons unique to the learning profile of each student. Before meeting with the students, the candidates observe a demonstration at the elementary school. The instructors demonstrate typical assessment administration, strategy lesson implementation, and record-keeping behavior for the candidates with a student who will participate in the clinic.

The Sessions

During the following week candidates begin meeting with identified at-risk students one-on-one after school, from 4:15 to 5:15 and 5:30 to 6:30. They instruct the same student for some 11–13 sessions, encompassing formal and ongoing assessment; structured lessons related to reading, word study, and writing; short read-alouds; and homework. The research-based lesson structure (Clay, 1991; Dorn et al., 1998; Fountas & Pinnell, 2000; Morris, 2002) consists of four components: (1) rereading a familiar book or passage, (2) reading a new book or passage, (3) word study, and (4) writing.

After the second session ends, at 6:30 P.M., the instructor, supervisor, and reading specialist candidates continue their seminar coursework until 8:00 P.M. by discussing their students' reading behaviors and reflecting on students' progress, their own teaching behaviors and methods, praxis, and balanced reading instruction and strategy use.

DEVELOPING PROGRAMS FOR AT-RISK READERS

The RIS program and the literacy learning clinic are two examples of intervention programs developed by literacy leaders to meet the needs of those students who struggle the most with reading. The programs are described in an effort to support other literacy leaders in creating programs for their own districts and schools.

Developing a program to support at-risk readers does take time and commitment, but isn't necessarily difficult. Certain similar features in common between the two intervention programs described in this chapter are that they are grounded in research and experience and replicated in exemplary intervention programs. But before undertaking even the first step, one must be certain that they key administrators involved support the idea of an intervention program and that enough educators and literacy leaders in one's community are willing to join together in making a long term commitment to the students who will benefit from the program.

ORGANIZING AN INITIAL MEETING TO CREATE AN INTERVENTION PROGRAM

One begins by organizing an initial meeting with administrators, reading specialists, colleagues, and possibly even a PTA representative to discuss the specific program one conceives to support those considered at risk or struggling in the area of reading. The agenda for such a meeting might include:

- When the program would take place (before, during, or after school).
- Where the instructors and students would meet.
- Who the instructors would be (teachers, volunteers, high schoolers, reading specialist candidates).
- The estimated costs.

The first meeting might also undertake the naming of a program coordinator, provision for materials, determination of student selection criteria, and selecting program meeting dates and times.

Once the program coordinator is named, an appointed committee can begin creating the intervention program. The committee will also need to arrange for instructor training sessions that reflect the unique needs of the students and the school. Training that is most successful includes ongoing instruction that provides ample time for reflection and evaluation. Those who both instruct and participate in ongoing training are more likely to return to the program year after year (Blachowicz et al., 2006).

The remainder of this chapter expands on the topics of student eligibility, assessment, lesson planning, teacher–student rapport, and communication as they relate to intervention programs. Literacy leaders should consider these areas carefully as they embark on creating and implementing an intervention program. Because there is such a wide selection of excellent reference sources on intervention, tutoring, and volunteer programs, those topics will not be treated here; however, resources are cited at the end of this chapter (see Appendix 3.1) for further information on those subjects.

To begin, let us consider which students might benefit most from a reading intervention program.

Determining Whom to Include in the Reading Program

Most reading programs must limit their number of enrollees based on the number of teaching associates available. Thus, there must be clear data-driven criteria to determine who is eligible for participation. Most students are invited on the basis of standardized test scores as well classroom-based formal and informal assessments. Prescribing a range of requisite scores on standardized and formal assessments helps classroom teachers decide who is most in need of additional assistance. Then, among those who meet the initial criteria, informal assessment can add useful information about various individuals' special strengths and challenges.

Using the assembled data (see Table 3.1 for a sample), teachers should meet in grade-level groups with literacy leaders to determine which students should be invited to participate. Based on our experience, students should be selected based on grade level rather than allowing each classroom teacher to choose a specified number of children to participate. Thus, one teacher in a given grade level might have three children participating in an intervention program while another might have only one—but what we have found is that this is the best way to support those most in need of additional reading support. Furthermore, this approach to selection targets the students with "serious, pervasive reading disabilities" (Bursuck & Damer, 2007, p. 3).

Assessment

Any reading intervention program should always begin with assessment, end with assessment, and include ongoing assessment. In addition to the data provided by the classroom teacher, assessments provide data to develop and implement an instructional plan customized to the student's unique strengths and challenges.

At the beginning of a reading intervention program, an initial battery of assessments defines a baseline, or starting point, from which the student will progress. Ongoing informal and formal evaluation of student progress during each tutoring session

TABLE 3.1. Organizing Assessment Data to Determine Reading Program Participants in Fourth Grade

Student name	State test Far below basic 150–268	Informal reading inventory Instructional level	Rate	Spelling inventory Score	Level	Reading attitude survey Recreational	Academic
Alec	200	1st	45 wcpm	10/25	Long-vowel patterns	25/40	20/40
Jesnee	256	2nd	66 wcpm	13/25	Other vowel patterns	33/40	30/40
Taylor	160	1st	39 wcpm	8/25	Long-vowel patterns	22/40	12/40

Note. wcpm, words correctly read per minute.

affects both the immediate and longer-term instruction, allowing for accelerated learning. When (1) it is the end of the academic year or (2) a student "graduates" from the intervention program, the same battery of assessments that was administered as the initial battery should be repeated to document growth and improvement. We also recommend that the battery of tests be administered in January for all struggling and at-risk readers.

The Assessment Battery

The pre- and postassessment battery should help one glean the most useful information about the student's knowledge of orthography, syntax, semantics, phonological awareness/phonics, comprehension, vocabulary, and reading fluency. In other words, the battery should include assessments that cover (1) the spelling system and letter patterns, (2) the way sentences and words function in English, (3) word meanings along with how words are used within the context of a text, (4) letter combinations and letter sounds along with letter–sound relationships, (5) monitoring and reading for meaning, and (6) the ability to read fluently at an appropriate rate and with understanding. Another key metric to ascertain is student's attitude toward reading.

The battery of assessments we recommend offers a thorough review of both students' strengths and challenges, or weaknesses. This battery includes a spelling inventory, an informal reading inventory (IRI), a reading attitude survey, a writing sample, and, for those reading primary grade-level texts, the Observation Survey (Clay, 2006). Table 3.2 explains the benefits of using each assessment type and lists specific recommendations.

Berrill, Doucette, and Verhulst (2006) note that it is also important to assess whether students understand that a text's print type can contribute to comprehension. For example, students need to know that words may be printed in boldface or italic fonts for specific reasons, that prose text looks and is read differently from poetry text, and that headings in informational text shouldn't be ignored. A given text's font type may be a pragmatic cue (p. 9) that many struggling readers ignore and thus the oversight needs to be assessed and addressed by means of instruction.

There is a simple way to develop an assessment tool to determine whether students are aware of these traditional print conventions. Using a grade-level content area textbook such as social studies or science, flag pages that include (1) headings and subheadings, (2) words in boldface and italic fonts, and (3) quoted material and bullets. Older students' assessments should include an evaluation of their use of tables, figures and other graphic elements and margin notes and notations. Students are then asked questions similar to "What is different here [in the type of print]? Why did the author include this? How can it help you as a reader?" Figure 3.3 is a sample of a Text Appearance Assessment Record Sheet that can be used as a guide in creating an assessment tool for the textbooks used in school.

TABLE 3.2. Suggestions for a Pre- and Postassessment Battery

Assessment	Why include it?	Recommendations
Spelling inventory	Spelling features are assessed to determine which aspects are known, unknown, and/or used incorrectly.	Bear, Invernizzi, Templeton, & Johnston (2007); Schlagel (1982)
Informal reading inventory	Administered one-on-one, IRIs assess word accuracy, vocabulary, comprehension, and fluency. Independent, instructional, and frustration reading levels are determined. Students' uses of reading strategies may also be observed.	Basic Reading Inventory (Johns, 2008); Qualitative Reading Inventory–5 (Leslie & Caldwell, 2010)
Reading attitude survey	Surveys offer information on reading attitudes, enabling teachers to consider various materials and types of instruction.	*www.professorgarfield.org/ parents_teachers/printables/pdfs/ reading/readingsurvey.pdf* or McKenna and Kear (1990) *www.readwritethink.org/lesson_ images/lesson110/attitude.pdf*
Writing samples	Writing samples are used to determine the skills of the writer, along with which skills are consistent, in development, and/or in need of support.	Spandel (2007, 2008); *www. readwritethink.org/lesson_images/ lesson782/Rubric.pdf*
Observation Survey	Tasks include letter identification by name or sound, word reading, concepts about language represented in print, writing words, phonemic awareness, and text reading with a running record. Although the survey was developed to assess emergent readers, some tasks may be helpful in assessing older struggling readers or English language learners.	Clay (2006)

Ongoing Assessment

Ongoing assessment is particularly important for accelerated learning and teaching effectiveness. During each session at least one running record, or analysis of miscues, should be included for either a familiar or an unfamiliar passage reading, if not both. Running records and miscue analyses are examined and evaluated to guide the instructor's planning and teaching, both in the current and subsequent sessions. A checklist of story grammar components can help with ongoing comprehension assessment by documenting an unaided or prompted retelling of what was read, and strategy use can be documented in anecdotal observations of reading behaviors. When assessing reading fluency,

Name: _____   Grade: _____   Date: _____

Textbook Title: *Earth Science*

Text Feature	Example	Questions	Student Response
Boldface Type	Your senses help to gather information about the world, allowing for **observation**. (Textbook, page 3)	What is different here? Why did the author include boldface print? How can it help you as a reader?	
Bullets	To help understand the world around you, you need to • Observe by using the five senses. • Interpret the observation by inferring. • Predict by using what you know about the world. (Textbook, page 4)	What are these? Why did the author include them? How can they help you as a reader?	
Tables	Table 1: Science Skills (Textbook, page 3)	What is this? Why did the author include it? How can it help you as a reader?	
Graphic Organizer	Scientific Inquiry Cycle (Textbook, page 4)	What is this? Why did the author include it? How can it help you as a reader?	
Italics	In a thunderstorm, *don't* stay near trees because the lightening may strike the trees and then you. (Textbook, page 137)	What is different here? Why did the author include this type of print? How can it help you as a reader?	
Headings and Subheadings	Heading: Tornadoes Subheadings: What Are Tornadoes? Being Safe in a Tornado (Textbook, pages 136–137)	What are these? Why did the author include them? How can they help you as a reader?	
Quotation Marks	"Tornado alley" is located in the middle of the United States. (Textbook, page 138)	What are these? Why did the author include them? How can they help you as a reader?	
Figure	Figure 10: A Tornado Forms (Textbook, page 137)	What is this? Why did the author include it? How can it help you as a reader?	
Margin Notes	A Tornado in a Jar (Textbook, page 135)	What is this? Why did the author include it? How can it help you as a reader?	

FIGURE 3.3. Sample of a Text Appearance Assessment Record Sheet.

it is vital to include a fluency scale to record prosody in addition to reporting accuracy and the words correctly read per minute (wcpm) rate (Moskal & Blachowicz, 2006). Ongoing assessment for understanding and automaticity in word study usually includes a written "test" of the concepts students learned—initial sounds, spelling patterns, or spelling rules, for example. Writing samples are reviewed first by the student and then together with the instructor to record which writing goals are met consistently, which are still in progress, and whether new goals need to be set.

Records of ongoing assessment can be kept in a binder with each session's lesson plans. Charts (see Figures 3.4 and 3.5 for examples) are also used to document progress over time and to be able to quickly survey students' progress. The charts document what the student learned and continues to learn but can also be used to help intervention instructors collaborate with the classroom teachers to ensure that each is supporting the instruction of the other.

Lesson Planning

Planning the lesson is one of the most important steps in ensuring a well-organized, effective session that stays focused and keeps the student (and the instructor) on task. It can be thought of as a map of the session that provides flexibility when necessary. The lesson plan depicted in Figure 3.6 is simply a suggestion, as the plan can be formatted to satisfy the needs of any reading intervention program.

The four target areas are listed across the top of the lesson plan. These areas—Familiar Reading, New Reading, Word Study, and Writing—are found in some form in many research-based reading intervention or tutoring programs. To begin, each text and its corresponding reading level are recorded in the Familiar and New Reading sections, while the lesson's focus is recorded in the Word Study and Writing sections. Following that, each target area has a place to add the more specific area of reading the student is

Date	Title and Level	Accuracy	Self-Correction Rate	Number of Meaning Changes	Independent, Instructional, or Frustration	Comments on Meaning, Structure, Visual, and Cross-Checking	Fluency Rate and Rubric Score
Nov. 1	The Egypt Game / U Synder [1967]	342/370 92%	1:6	0	Instructional	Still relies heavily on visual cues and occasionally on meaning.	95 wcpm 2

FIGURE 3.4. Running record history used for ongoing assessment. Accuracy calculation is the words read correctly, divided by the total number of words. The self-correction calculation is (number of errors + number of self-corrections), divided by the number of self-corrections, expressed as the ratio of 1: (the answer to the equation, rounded to the nearest whole number).

Date	Writing Goal	New Writing Features Observed	Writing Features In Development	Writing Features to Introduce in the Next Session
Nov. 7	To use a graphic organizer to assist in organizing a draft and then use the graphic organizer when writing.	• Began to create paragraphs without a reminder. • Used the graphic organizer today with less resistance.	• Still working on paragraph development. • Still encouraging revision.	Indent paragraphs (but not in the next session).

FIGURE 3.5. Writing history used for ongoing assessment.

"working on" and the lesson's objective, which states what the student should be able to do upon completion of the assignment.

Next there is a Lesson Description for each of the four target areas. *Areas to revisit* is listed in Familiar Reading to remind the instructor of what needs to be reviewed for practice or observed for mastery. *Strategy to practice* is listed in New Reading to document which specific word recognition, comprehension, or fluency strategy is to be practiced by the reader. In all target areas, *Before*, *During*, and *After* are listed. This listing enables the instructor to better prepare a comprehensive and well-scaffolded lesson that anticipates what will be used to introduce the lesson, what will be accomplished throughout the lesson, and what will bring it to a conclusion or connect it to the next lesson. We urge instructors to anticipate and state their purposes and goals in all four target areas so that students can explicitly see and understand the interconnectedness of the readings and assignments.

A section for the instructor's observations follows. This space is where the instructor can jot down anecdotal notes and document reading behaviors to chronicle change, progress, or the lack thereof. Following the observation section is a place to record a recommended book that should be read aloud to the student simply for enjoyment. With students who struggle, it is crucial that they listen to books read aloud that are truly interesting to them, at their own comprehension level but not too difficult to read, and readily available independently. This added incentive to read is especially important for upper elementary and older students who are unable to access the books their peers are reading.

Finally, homework practice is an integral part of reading intervention programs. Repeating at home what is practiced in the program supports and crucially reinforces proficiency and automaticity. Some instructors avoid using the word homework because so many students think "homework stinks," and instead they prefer to describe the work for home as practice. "Practice" appears to be more inviting to students than "homework." An example of a completed plan is shown in Figure 3.7.

As mentioned earlier, this lesson plan is simply a possible outline and can be changed. The plan in Figure 3.7 is formatted for individual instruction, while the lesson

Student: _____ Session: _____ Date: _____

FAMILIAR READING	NEW READING	WORD STUDY	WRITING
Text Name/Level:	**Text Name/Level:**	**Focus:**	**Focus:**
Areas to revisit:	**Working on:**	**Working on:**	**Working on:**
Upon completion, the student should be able to:	**Upon completion, the student should be able to:**	**Upon completion, the student should be able to:**	**Upon completion, the student should be able to:**
Lesson Description **Before:** **During:** **After:**	**Lesson Description** **Strategy to practice:** **Before:** **During:** **After:**	**Lesson Description** **Before:** **During:** **After:**	**Lesson Description** **Before:** **During:** **After:**

(cont.)

FIGURE 3.6. Possible lesson plan outline for a reading intervention program.

FAMILIAR READING	NEW READING	WORD STUDY	WRITING
Observations	**Observations**	**Observations**	**Observations**

Read Aloud:

Practice at Home:

FIGURE 3.6. *(cont.)*

Student: <u>Melissa</u>   Session: <u>10</u>   Date: <u>12/10</u>

FAMILIAR READING	NEW READING	WORD STUDY	WRITING
Text Name/Level: The Egypt Game [Snyder, 1967] Level U, pp. 22–23	**Text Name/Level:** The Egypt Game Level U, pp. 34–41	**Focus:** Sorting with automaticity	**Focus:** Paragraph development
Areas to revisit: Appropriate phrasing Pausing at periods	**Working on:** DR-TA, setting a purpose for reading, developing a "right there" question (QAR)	**Working on:** adding suffixes to words with short and long vowels	**Working on:** All sentences in one paragraph are about one idea.
Upon completion, the student should be able to: read with appropriate phrasing on the second reading.	**Upon completion, the student should be able to:** create a "right there" question.	**Upon completion, the student should be able to:** complete a Spell Check on the whiteboard with 80% accuracy.	**Upon completion, the student should be able to:** write one paragraph that stays focused on one idea.
Lesson Description	**Lesson Description**	**Lesson Description**	**Lesson Description**
Rereads passage silently, followed by a fluent read-aloud **Before:** "On which aspect of fluency are you working? What can you do to phrase properly?" **During:** She reads silently and then aloud. **After:** She self-assesses and rereads if necessary.	Focus on reading for meaning **Strategy to practice:** DR-TA, QAR **Before:** Review predictions and write a new one. Vocabulary: accumulated, p. 35 hieroglyphics, p. 35 out of the ordinary, p. 38 **During:** Use post-it notes to mark new words and wonderings. **After:** Go over post-it notes, predictions, and question.	Looking to see if she is ready for a new suffix sort **Before:** Tell me about the sort. **During:** Watch for automaticity. **After:** If she sorted all correctly do a Spell Check on a whiteboard. If not, have her correct the errors.	She writes a minimum of one paragraph in response to the Egypt Game chapter. **Before:** Review the formation of a paragraph **During:** Assist if necessary **After:** She reads, comments on what was done well. Is it focused on one topic? How do you know? Is there anything that needs to be revised?
Observations	**Observations**	**Observations**	**Observations**
She was able to read with correct phrasing and pause at the periods. She knew she did well!	Her predictions incorporated what she read in the prior chapter. She feels more comfortable marking words with which she is unfamiliar.	She sorted correctly and got all right on the Spell Check. She is ready for the new sort. She was very confident throughout.	This continues to be a challenge. She does not seem to be able to organize her writing. I need to again consider a graphic organizer for response writing.

Read Aloud:
Continue Thief of Hearts [Yep, 1995], starting at p. 27.

Practice at Home:
Suffix sort; read pp. 42–49 of The Egypt Game; use post-it notes to jot down unknown or interesting words; prepare two "right there" questions and one "author and me" question.

FIGURE 3.7. Possible lesson plan outline for a reading intervention program.

plan shown in Figure 3.8 is formatted for small-group instruction. In the small-group plan the observation section is different, thereby permitting the instructor to comment on each student in the group.

Developing Rapport

One of the key ways to ensure success when working with at-risk readers is to develop a sense of rapport with them based on mutual trust (Morris, 2005). Although trust can sometimes take a while to develop, those working with struggling readers can begin to

Students: Marco, Mandeep, Rianna, Sam   Session: _____   Date: _____

FAMILIAR READING	NEW READING	WORD STUDY	WRITING
Text Name/Level: Areas to revisit: Upon completion, the student should be able to:	Text Name/Level: Working on: Upon completion, the student should be able to:	Focus: Working on: Upon completion, the student should be able to:	Focus: Working on: Upon completion, the student should be able to:
Lesson Description Before: During: After:	Lesson Description Strategy to practice: Before: During: After:	Lesson Description Before: During: After:	Lesson Description Before: During: After:
Observations			
Marco	Mandeep	Rianna	Sam
Read Aloud:			
Practice at Home:			

FIGURE 3.8. Reading intervention program lesson plan sample developed for small-group instruction.

create a positive relationship even at the first meeting by talking with the students about their interests, reading behaviors, what they do well, and what they believe can help them become better readers. It is also essential to believe that the students can progress and to share that conviction with them not only at the first meeting but throughout the relationship (Berrill et al., 2006; Gillespie & Lerner, 2008; Gordon, 2005).

Working as learning partners or a team can also help to create good rapport. Positive feedback and being interested, compassionate, and empathetic set up conditions where students will try new strategies, risk failure, and feel motivated to do their best (Gordon, 2005). And although you seek to build a student–instructor learning partnership, it is essential that this relationship eventually lead to the student's own self-reliance. The primary goal of good rapport is to build the confidence of those at risk to prove that they can *independently* implement the good reading strategies they've been taught. In other words, instructors help students to see that they are self-sufficient and *don't need* to rely on anyone other than themselves to be a good reader (Wisker, Exley, Antoniou, & Ridley, 2008).

Communication

Communication among all those involved with the reading progress of students is essential to accelerate the learning process. Parents, guardians, and teachers who communicate frequently with one another create an environment that promotes deeper understanding of each student's strengths and challenges as well as support positive reading behaviors and habits. We recommend, as do Berrill et al. (2006), that instructors assisting struggling readers in any intervention program communicate with both the parents and the classroom teachers at least once a week.

Communication with teachers and parents can take on many forms. E-mail is a fast and convenient way to mention a few highlights from the sessions and any consistent progress observed. E-mail is also a practical method of recording communications for a student's file. Since students bring reading activities home to practice between sessions, adding a note to this work is another convenient way to communicate with parents about what was accomplished during the session and what is important to practice. Older students aren't always eager to share what they need to practice; so, an alternative is a parent sign-off sheet added to the practice work taken home and returned at the next session, followed up with a text message reminder to both the student and parent.

Classroom teachers also appreciate being contacted, especially when the reading practice is not getting done at home. No only can classroom teachers reinforce to parents the importance of their children's completing the practice assignments, but also when the practice fails to be consistently completed at home, they can occasionally give students extra time in class to do the work. It is clearly in the student's best interest to practice, and the student must be made to realize the importance of getting it done.

Here are some suggestions for additional reading stimulation that instructors might usefully share with parents or teachers:

- Games that are used for word study, like Memory and Old Maid.
- Word patterns and sorting games that need to be practiced.
- Titles of interesting books at the student's instructional level for reading practice and enjoyment.
- Book titles at the student's interest level for read-aloud practices or books on CD.
- Comprehension question suggestions that promote reflection and making connections.
- Ideas for undertaking independent writing tasks at home.
- Any other concepts that need to be practiced, such as answering inferential questions or implementing strategies for understanding new vocabulary from the content.

IMPLEMENTING KEY IDEAS

In this chapter, we described two specific reading intervention programs—the reading intervention specialist (RIS) program and the Literacy Learning Clinic—created to support struggling readers. Suggestions for literacy leaders who wish to create similar intervention programs include:

- Building a team of literacy leaders, educators, and administrators to discuss organizing an intervention program and naming a coordinator.
- Reaching out to parent organizations or institutions of higher education for additional support.
- Establishing the eligibility criteria for student participants.
- Providing for formal, informal, and ongoing assessment practices.
- Organizing a coherent lesson plan.
- Building positive rapport between reading specialist instructors and students.
- Assuring consistently open channels of communication between classroom teachers, parents, and administrators.

CONCLUDING THOUGHTS

A final bit of advice for literacy leaders is to start with a pilot program in one grade level or emphasizing one area of concern, such as fluency (Blachowicz et al., 2006). By starting small, literacy leaders can develop an effective and consistent program, understand their limitations, learn from their mistakes, share their accomplishments, and gradually improve the program on a realistic time-line (Covey, 1989). Being part of a reading intervention program is a rewarding experience, for what can be better than helping struggling readers to improve?

APPENDIX 3.1. RESOURCES FOR DEVELOPING INTERVENTION PROGRAMS

Berrill, D., Doucette, C., & Verhulst, D. (2006). *Tutoring adolescent readers*. Markham, Ontario: Pembroke.

This book assists in developing a tutoring program for students ages 12–18. Suggestions are made for increasing motivation, supporting those who are learning English, and training beginning tutors. We especially like the sections on preparing students for the sessions and working with parents.

Johnson, A. P. (2008). *Teaching reading and writing: A guidebook for tutoring and remediating students*. Lanham, MD: Rowman & Littlefield Education.

This book includes effective literacy strategies and advice on how to create a dynamic program with a small budget. We particularly like that the authors stress the importance of using books that motivate students to read; in particular, they encourage the use of comic books, cartoon strips, and graphic novels to develop students' interest in reading.

Morris, D. (2005). *The Howard Street tutoring manual: Teaching at-risk readers in the primary grades* (2nd ed.). New York: Guilford Press.

This manual is a valuable tool for tutors who work with beginning readers. Key sections address the recruitment of volunteers, reading assessments, program effectiveness, and the case studies included help one understand how best to set up instructional sessions and measure student progress.

Wisker, G., Exley, K., Antoniou, M., & Ridley, P. (2008). *Working one-to-one with students: Supervising, coaching, mentoring, and personal tutoring*. New York: Routledge.

This short book offers guidance, resources, and case studies along with theory to build a program that supports students. We endorse the book's emphasis on the importance of ensuring students' success by "building their capacity to help themselves" (p. 137).

PART II

LITERACY LEADERSHIP WITH SPECIFIC STUDENT GROUPINGS

CHAPTER FOUR

Boys and Reading in School
A Different Kind of Struggle

When Juliet informs Romeo that he is kissing "by the book,"
she is not complimenting him on his literacy.

—THOMAS NEWKIRK

Will's mom, a private tutor and retired reading specialist, drove him home from school one early October afternoon. He was still getting tired after a full day of first grade, and she reconsidered her plans to go to the library. "Will, I was thinking of stopping at the library on the way home. What do you think?" Will perked up at the thought, "Can we go? I want to go! I need to get some books."

At the library, Will headed straight for the *Judy and Stink Moody* series by Megan McDonald (*www.judymoody.com/#books*). He knew exactly where the series was located. He took a book he had not yet read and walked around the corner to the shelves of comic books. He selected a Garfield book and leaned against the wall. He opened the book and read what he could, giggling every now and then.

After checking out their selections of hardcover books and audiobooks, Will and his mom listened to *Cricket in Times Square* (Selden, 1960) in the car. When they arrived home, Will's mom took his backpack from the trunk and asked about his day. Will mentioned that he had to stay in for recess again to complete his reading worksheets.

"I had to hide my anger," Will's mom explained later. "Why would anyone want to keep an active 6-year-old boy in for recess to finish reading worksheets when this could keep him from being able to sit still and stay engaged for the long afternoon? You know that worksheets don't teach how to read, *and* the child obviously loves reading! I remember this day clearly because I could no longer let the missed recesses continue. I made an appointment with the teacher and told her, as respectfully as I could, that my son was not to be kept in for recess. Any work that needed to be done was to be sent home for homework. And so began a 5-year struggle I didn't foresee: the struggle of my bibliophile son with the school's reading curriculum."

Will's home life and preschool experiences were immersed in language and literacy. He went to first grade ready to learn, but the literacy curriculum didn't sustain his interest. He wasn't motivated to fill in worksheets, and he rebelled against the hamburger structure (i.e., bun/contents/bun = topic sentence/details/concluding sentence) he was forced to use when writing. He had little voice in choosing reading and writing topics and didn't value many of the assignments he was asked to complete (Smith & Wilhelm, 2006). Will and many of his male classmates were struggling to make sense of literacy at school.

This chapter explores boys' special struggles with the literacy curriculum in schools along with research that begins to explain the reasons for these struggles. Suggestions on how to engage boy readers (and writers) are offered by researchers, experts, and Will himself. But, first, back to the story about Will.

"I finally realized what was happening with Will's literacy education in the final weeks of first grade," Will's mom remembered. "I had returned from the International Reading Association Conference, and I was unpacking the books that I brought home for him. After inspecting the pile, he whispered in my ear, 'Mom, you know I hate reading.' My stomach instantly ached, and I'm sure I turned white.

"Almost a week later I found the books I had given Will from IRA. He had a stack of trade books next to his bed but none were the books that were obviously intended for reading instruction—and with that I finally understood what Will had really said to me. He didn't hate *reading*, the activity; rather, he hated "reading," the subject taught in school. Will saw no connection between reading at home and reading at school—*and how could he?* There really *was* no connection! At home, reading was a pleasurable, authentic experience in which literature was discussed, while at school reading was not pleasurable, not discussed, and far from authentic."

This disconnect between reading at home and reading at school appears to be a common phenomenon (Smith & Wilhelm, 2006; Sullivan, 2009). Smith and Wilhelm (2006) noted that the young men in their study drew a line between their home lives and school lives and made no connections between the literature read at school and their own lives. One student went so far as to use different words to describe reading that took place at home ("lookin' at the newspaper") and "reading" that took place at school (p. 25). Since reading is intended to be a potentially transformative meaning-making experience, why isn't real reading happening for boys at school?

In general, males still score below females in reading. The Nation's Report Card (National Assessment of Educational Progress, 2010) showed that in 2009 eighth-grade boys scored an average of 259 on a 500-point scale, while females scored 269 (0.3 standard error). Fourth-grade boys scored 218 while the girls scored 224 (0.3 standard error). Reading scores from 2007 to 2009 stayed the same for fourth-grade males, while scores for eighth-grade males increased by one point. Clearly, there is an achievement gap for males in reading.

Neu and Weinfeld (2007) explain that in education boys can become lost because their natural character isn't acknowledged. When the school system doesn't consider boys' interests or build on their interests, it is more difficult for boys to achieve. Furthermore, teachers tend to reject the kinds of stories boys like to read and write—that is, ones featuring action, violence, and twisted humor—and in doing so, they tend to turn boys off (Fletcher, 2006; Guzzetti, Young, Gritsavage, Fyfe, & Hardenbrook, 2002; Newkirk, 2002).

On average, boys spend less time reading than girls, and this disparity of time spent on task creates a major barrier to their success in school (Goldberg & Roswell, 2002; Neu & Weinfeld, 2007; Sullivan, 2009). Of course, as just noted, in many classrooms boys are not allowed to engage meaningfully with many of the topics that most naturally interest them. The literate world of boys is less well known or accepted by (predominantly female) teachers in schools, but thankfully this predisposition is beginning to undergo change. Increasingly, literacy leaders are trying to develop more boy-friendly literacy practices (without shortchanging the needs of girls).

HELPING BOYS TO REJOICE IN LITERACY

Given that so many researchers, authors, and teachers are actively investigating the area of boys in relation to education, literacy leaders may very usefully rethink how male students generally interact with literacy in the schools. In this next section, current trends in the research on boys and reading are reviewed.

Finding What Gets Boys Excited

Determining what most excites boys' imagination is important to helping them broaden their interests and views of the world (Sullivan, 2009). Reading on subjects of high interest is naturally motivating (Neu & Weinfeld, 2007) and has been known to stimulate reading undertaken for the sheer pleasure of it. Surveys and self-reports are an excellent way to gather relevant data on this issue, and one example is given in Figure 4.1. This example includes suggestions from a group of 11- and 12-year-old boys when solicited for advice on what a teacher should ask to gather information about what excites and interests them. It was encouraging to see that some of the questions directly related to reading even though reading was not mentioned when speaking with them.

Interest Survey for Boys

Name (optional): _____   Date: _____

1. List three (or more) things you like to do. _____

   _____

   _____

   _____

2. Your favorite Internet site is _____

   because: _____

   _____

   _____

3. Your favorite video game is _____

   because: _____

   _____

   _____

4. List three (or more) music selections on your play list. _____

   _____

   _____

   _____

5. List the names of three (or more) authors you know and like. _____

   _____

   _____

   _____

6. Which reading genres interest you? Circle all that apply.

mystery	action and adventure	science fiction	fantasy
biography	nonfiction/information	realistic fiction	poetry
humor	graphic novels	historic fiction	other: _____

FIGURE 4.1. An example of an interest survey developed specifically for boys.

Once the relevant data are assembled, teachers are urged to gather together all kinds of reading materials related to the students' expressed interests. School librarians are always willing to assist in developing a rotating library collection that will offer a variety of reading genres and interesting topics over the course of the academic year. Librarians in public libraries are also very happy to assemble monthly "book bags" for classroom distribution.

Getting Those Boys Reading

So, you are asking, "How do I get the boys to read now that I have gathered appealing reading materials?" One way is Sustained Silent Reading (SSR) (Pilgreen, 2000). Although it has fallen out of favor with the recent increase emphasis on testing and assessment, pleasure reading in school—especially for boys and most especially for boys in middle and high school—deserves much greater allotments of time.

Buck (2010) has drawn attention to the importance of SSR in high school. She was dismayed to find that her 12th-grade students read only assigned books and knew that this could be contributing to declining reading scores (National Endowment for the Arts, 1997, 2004, 2007). Research has found that from 1992 to 2002 18- to 24-year-olds in general had a –20 percent decline in literary reading, the "steepest rate of decline in reading since the NEA survey history began" (National Endowment for the Arts, 2009, p. 4). From 1982 to 2002, males' literature reading declined at a higher rate than females' (National Endowment for the Arts, 2009). Stotsky (2006) has observed persuasively that if decreases in reading are a function of how the curriculum has evolved, then the curriculum must be changed.

To ensure that students read more frequently for enjoyment, Buck (2010) conducted an experiment by starting each English class with a period of SSR. In September, students began silent reading when the bell rang to start class and continued until the preset time was up, averaging some 50 minutes, in all, per week. Students self-selected their reading materials, with only textbooks and novels for English or literature classes disallowed. During this set period of time, Buck also engaged in SSR herself.

Buck (2010) found that students stayed engaged with their reading 91% of the time. They were discreetly observed twice a week, and although there was no significant increase in reading attitude by January, Buck observed that the students were actively engaged in reading and "did not mind reading during class" (p. 34). She also observed that most students completed reading books they started during SSR, they discussed what they were reading informally, and they readily exchanged book recommendations with their classmates.

This authentic reading time proved to motivate these 12th graders to read. This scheduled period was truly a time for pleasure reading without the journaling, testing, or book report assignments that, for example, make boys—especially—view reading as work (Guzzetti et al., 2002; Smith & Wilhelm, 2006). Students more actively sought out the classroom and school libraries, some borrowing books that Buck had read and recommended. Although Buck did not implement the SSR period specifically for her male students, they certainly read more than they would have without the SSR time.

Another way is to increase reading for enjoyment is to involve families in reading for pleasure at home. McCormick (2010) found that when fathers consciously read for pleasure in front of or with their boys, those boys' motivation for reading increased significantly. It is important to note that she also found that mothers helped increase motivation, and the affect was found for girls too.

Suspecting that families' beliefs about recreational reading could prove central to developing lifelong readers (Guzzetti et al., 2002; Tyre, 2008), McCormick (2010) created a program to encourage parents—but especially dads (or other male role models)—to get into the daily habit of both reading with their children and reading for themselves. Watching their key role models exhibit positive reading behaviors sends a powerful message to boys; namely, that reading is both masculine and gratifying (Neu & Weinfeld, 2007). In her study, McCormick (2010) simply asked that parents (particularly the fathers) increase the reading they were already doing by 5 minutes a day. This sole requirement meant that 10 minutes of reading would be increased to 15, and if there were no prior established reading habits, 5 minutes a day would be fine, to start. To track their consistency, moms and dads were encouraged to keep separate logs documenting the amount of time spent reading with or in front of their children. The insistence on separate logs was intended to impress upon the dads that their reading had a real and measurable impact on their children and that reading was not meant just for moms (McCormick, 2010).

Each week an e-mail was sent to all of the kindergarten, first- and second-grade parents to keep them connected and encouraged. These e-mails suggested ways to engage in literature discussions, find interesting materials, and increase their own reading (see Figures 4.2 and 4.3 for the e-mails' text).

Knowing that parents were more likely to stay involved if they could choose the materials they read, McCormick recommended not only fiction but also nonfiction and informational texts for authentic, enjoyable reading, like the sports page, comics, web pages, magazines, blogs, recipes, e-mails, brochures, and even manuals. She encouraged dads to read in front of their children rather than alone as some men do (Sullivan, 2009), and asked them to deliberately refer to what they were doing as "reading." Sullivan (2009) asserts that having boys observe their fathers reading newspapers doesn't really qualify as "watching reading," but many would disagree. Reading is reading, and boys can use reading as a way to learn and celebrate who they are and who they might be (Zambo & Brozo, 2009).

Book Recommendations

Although most girls would readily accept a book recommendation from a teacher, many boys would not. Neu and Weinfeld (2007) found that boys generally resist female teachers' book recommendations. While valuing book recommendations from males, especially peers, simply leaving reading selections around for boys to discover was the best way to entice them into reading.

Dear Families,

First of all, I want to thank all of you for your willingness to participate in this program. Motivating children to read is a very important matter for me, and I'm eager to begin our work together and make a difference. I'm really excited to have your support, and I appreciate your time and energy.

I'm enlisting all of you to modify your home reading habits. Basically, I'm asking you to increase the amount of leisure time reading you do every day at home in the presence of your child by a minimum of 5 minutes each day. I understand that your days are very busy and that most of the reading you do probably occurs when the kids are in bed and you have time to yourself. Nonetheless, the purpose of this reading program is to change an image of inaction to action so that there can be an impact on your child's impressions of the value of reading and on his or her motivation to read.

I'm encouraging not just one parent to participate but BOTH parents in two-parent households. Research shows that, more frequently than not, it is the mother who reads most frequently with the kids and is observed engaging in leisure-time reading. Considering the chronically lower levels of reading motivation and reading achievement among boys, I am asking that you provide a model of *both* parents reading at home so that your child can associate reading with everyday activities that you both value and enjoy. Like every other value, lesson, and moral that we share with our children, the way reading is modeled is absorbed by them. This is our opportunity to see if the cliché "Do as I say, not as I do" can be turned around to create a home environment where parents not only encourage reading but also support it by actively participating in reading during their own free time.

Here is your assignment: increase the amount of leisure-time reading (whether of newspapers, magazines, novels, or Internet articles) that you do in the *presence* of your child every day by at least 5 minutes. More time than that would be great, but I am asking for at least 5 minutes each day. I understand that some days do not provide the opportunity for reading, so please try to "make up" lost minutes for any days you may miss on other days of the week. For example, if you worked late or had a meeting to attend on Tuesday, make up for the lost reading time of Tuesday by reading at least 10 minutes on Wednesday.

Every Monday I will send a reading log to you via e-mail. The first reading log is attached to this e-mail. You can choose to track your reading every day and save the information or reflect back on your reading on Sunday. On the following Monday you will then e-mail the reading log back to me, one for each participating parent, and begin the tracking of your reading for the following week, much like your child completes a reading log in the classroom.

Obviously if you received this e-mail, I have at least one e-mail address for your family. If both parents in your household are able to participate, I would appreciate e-mail addresses for each parent. When sending me additional e-mail addresses, please make note of your child's name as well for my record keeping.

I will also be including reading strategy and skill ideas to support the ways that you and your child can read when I send out the weekly reading logs. I hope that you find these helpful, and I would love to have your input.

Happy reading!

FIGURE 4.2. The first weekly parent e-mail sample.

Will, whom you read about earlier in the chapter, suggests asking a librarian for help in selecting books, but he himself prefers to find recommendations on the Internet. Now in middle school, Will still reads for enjoyment when he isn't playing video games. He begins his search by seeking out specific genres, zeroing in on sites that include numerous book titles or annotated bibliographies. For example, he searches for "list of mystery books" and finds a variety of sites, such as *www.mysterynet.com/authors,* which catalogs the names of mystery writers and offers first chapters of selected titles. Once at the site, Will clicks on "Agatha Christie" to find her biological profile, background information on how some of her books came to be written, and listing of all of her authored titles.

Will also visits the library websites of major cities to get recommendations. The New York Public Library, at *www.nypl.org,* has "summer reading recommendations" cat-

Hello, Fantastic Parent Participants,

I hope that you continue to enjoy your increased reading time. I know that life is busy and comes at you rapid-fire, but I want you to know that your child is benefiting from your increasing your reading time.

I received last week's reading logs from a few overachievers who sent them in unsolicited (nicely done!). Please try to send your reading log to me by Tuesday night since I'm keeping track of the amount of leisure time reading. Please don't stress out if you didn't read every day—I'm not grading you! Of course, I'd love to see everyone reading frequently every night, but I'm a realist with two small children myself, and I understand that it's not always that simple. I'm hoping for an average of 5 minutes every night, but feel free to exceed that minimum number!

I am glad to have so many families with both parents participating. I encourage both parents to participate if you're in a two-parent household, and you can start even now. Both parents can submit their reading log at the same time if that's easier.

I received some questions asking if parents should track the minutes they read with their child in addition to the minutes they model reading. The answer is yes when the reading is done for leisure time, not for school work. Document any leisure time reading that you do in your house—maybe it's you with a magazine, newspaper, or book; maybe it's you and your child cozying up to read a favorite Roald Dahl book (just to throw out the name of a much-loved author). Focus on promoting reading as a valuable, enjoyable activity that you want to do. Discuss what you are reading, and share the ways that reading makes you think about things in new ways. As a parent, you play the most prominent role model in your child's life. You can help by sharing the way recreational reading connects to your life and makes you think. If your child sees you taking reading to this level, he or she is more likely to do the same.

I really enjoyed reading through your reading logs as they come in. Some of you shared anecdotes of new reading behaviors you're seeing in your child since the program began; while others are sharing strategies for getting in your reading time, such as using audiobooks during drives and taking family trips to the library for new inspiration. I hope that you are sharing with your child the reasons *why* you read. By "reasons," I don't mean citing this reading program but rather the underlying reason that you pick up a book, newspaper, or magazine or look at an Internet article. You do it to learn more about the world, challenge yourself to try new things, learn about new places, and even escape from your daily grind for a little bit.

Share with your child the connections that you make through your reading. Even beginning readers are able to grasp quite a bit and begin applying the lessons to their own reading. When they see you using reading as a useful tool, they will be more likely to do the same and hopefully will find a new value in reading that will stay with them throughout their life. Then, if you're feeling really daring, ask them what they think about their books and about the connections they make in their reading. Did the book or magazine article make them think of something that happened to them? Something from another book or movie? Something on the news or at school?

Shared reading (reading with your child) is a fantastic place to let them try this activity first. Read a chapter of a book like *Charlotte's Web* (White, 1952) or *The Fish in Room 11* (Dyer, 2004), and make a connection or two after reading it. Then, after you've modeled a few connections, challenge your child to make a connection *with* you. Once they get the hang of that, pull back and see if they can do it on their own. It's pretty cool once it starts happening.

One last resource I want to share with you today is *www.guysread.com*. Please check out this website. It's sponsored by a nonprofit organization headed by Jon Scieszka (an author kids love), whose mission is to motivate boys and men to read more by connecting them with really interesting reading selections. You'll find fantastic resources for boy-friendly book titles, interesting statistics on boys and reading, and information on encouraging male role models associated with reading. Click on that link, and I'm sure you'll be as excited about it as I am.

I thought I'd also mention two great books about reading to and with your child. The first is *How to Get Your Child to Love Reading* by Esme Raji Codell (2004), and the second is *The Read-Aloud Handbook* by Jim Trelease (2006). Both of these books highlight ways to engage with your child while reading with him or her, and how to pick books that will interest him or her, in addition to presenting an amazing list of titles. These two books are available at Amazon.com, but you can also get your hands on a copy in the local library, especially if you reserve it first online.

Thank you again for participating as we find ways to get our children motivated to read.

FIGURE 4.3. Weekly parent e-mail midprogram sample.

egorized by age level and includes recommended authors, series, and specific books, with the jacket covers pictured. The Chicago Public Library, at *www.chipublib.org*, includes recommended kid and teen titles on their main menu. The "For Teens" section includes the book title and jacket cover, reviews written by teenage peers, and a link to an annotated bibliography.

Reading Selections

Boys should have a wide variety of reading materials available from which to choose, including:

- Nonfiction
- Comics
- Newspapers
- Web pages
- Graphic novels
- Fiction that includes, for example:
  o Male protagonists
  o Action, adventure, courage, and determination
  o Humor
  o The creepy, weird, and shocking

Knowles and Smith (2005) insist that each classroom library should include at least one current copy of the *Guinness Book of World Records*, and we agree. We have seen well-loved copies of that volume shared over and over by boys in our own classrooms.

Brozo (2002) discusses the importance of emphasizing book selections that allow boys a natural entry point into reading such as the *Harry Potter* (*www.jkrowling.com*) and *Goosebumps* (*www.rlstine.com*) series. These texts were also made into movies or television series, supplying an additional visual component that is especially valuable to boys (Knowles & Smith, 2005; Smith & Wilhelm, 2006). Tatum (2009) stresses that entry point selections for adolescent boys should reflect their activities, interests, and sometimes confusing and uncomfortable stage of life. Scieszka (2005) notes that boys just need books that *they* want to read.

After the titles are selected, they need to be organized in an accessible way. Organizing a wide variety of book selections for boys in classroom libraries can be coordinated in a number of ways. In the primary grades, classroom libraries may be organized by reading level so that students are readily able to pick titles they are able to read. In the higher grades, books may be organized by genre, topic, or type (e.g., books, comics, magazines). Selections can be tagged as specifically recommended for boys, no matter what type of organizational scheme is used. Many teachers include an "I Recommend This Book" sheet on the inside cover (see Figure 4.4). These sheets stay in the book year after year and are frequently perused and taken into account when a title is being considered.

Recommendations for *True Stories of the Second World War* by P. Dowswell (2003)		
Name	Date	Comment
Vishal Abarci	9/10/10	Thrilling and unbelievable!
Cotey Ito	10/18/10	Be sure to read the introduction. Watch for a show about Iwo Jima on the Military Channel.

FIGURE 4.4. "I Recommend This Book" example.

We suggest in all grades that there be a section of the classroom library that changes over time where teachers can place materials for all reading levels from public libraries or their own personal libraries. We have seen students of all ages who are particularly interested in the books that are kept in the homes of their teachers. Mary Kay would sometimes have former students stop by her classroom just to look at or borrow the books on the shelf that housed her personal collection.

INSTRUCTIONAL STRATEGIES

Because reading is a meaning-making activity, boys especially need strategies to help them immerse themselves in increasingly deep levels of comprehension. The instructional strategies profiled here are research-based and recommended for boys (but also equally appropriate for girls). These strategies include book discussions (Daniels, 2002; Raphael & McMahon, 1997), Question Answer Relationships (QAR; Raphael, 1986), and think-alouds (Davey, 1983). We, of course, advocate for a large number of strategies that are successful with boys, but we choose to highlight these, having implemented them in our own classrooms and clinics with great success. It is not our intention to describe the strategies in great detail here, since they are well known to literacy leaders; we do, however, explain how they may look different through a boy-focused lens.

In general, Neu and Weinfeld (2007) found boys to be most engaged when new instructional strategies were introduced and practiced with texts that held their interest. Instructional literacy activities that were hands-on, multisensory, and that allowed for movement, challenge, and competition were apt to seem the most attractive and productive to boys (Knowles & Smith, 2005).

Book Discussions

Literature circles (Daniels, 2002) and book talks (Raphael & McMahon, 1997) are perfect vehicles to engage all readers. Literature circles and book talks involve discussion groups that respond to a reading, construct meaning about it, and enable readers to move to a deeper level of understanding through collaboration and critical thinking. Boys tend to engage better in book discussions when they are in a same-gender group and/or when the group is led by a male peer or adult (Smith & Wilhelm, 2006; Sullivan, 2009).

In book discussions, boys tend to take a more efferent stance (Guzzetti et al., 2002). They focus more on action and facts and less on multiple points of view and feelings, even when reading fiction. They also don't respond well to reading intended just to answer preset questions whose answers the teacher already knows, nor to reading aloud without practice or a chance to prepare in advance (Moskal & Blachowicz, 2006; Smith & Wilhelm, 2006; Zambo & Brozo, 2009). Finally, boys need to be told why they are engaging in book discussions since they don't always understand the meaning of the assignment (Rae & Pederson, 2007; Smith & Wilhelm, 2006). Once they understand, they are more inclined to fully participate and learn.

Book discussions are guided by meaningful questions to build on initial and developing understanding and to delve into what Langer (1995) calls "envisionment building," or the creation of a continuous personal interpretation of a text. Open-ended questions enable the group to build on individuals' understanding by exploring, rethinking, explaining, and defending. Along similar lines, Tatum (2009) stresses the use of "essential questions" (p. 90) in boys' discussions. Essential questions create talk about significant issues, inclining the individuals in the group to exchange their views and thereby forcing the consideration of multiple perspectives in creating understanding. Envisionment building and asking essential questions involve boys in book discussions that are engaging and motivating and can be incorporated into the Question Answer Relationship strategy.

Question Answer Relationships

Raphael (1986) developed the QAR strategy to help students understand the relationship between a question and its answer, specifying where and how to answer questions for maximum understanding. In QAR terms, questions and answers are divided into two major categories, namely, "In the Book" and "In My Head," specifying where answers may be found. "In the Book" includes (1) Right There and (2) Think and Search questions and answers. The answer to a literal question can be found Right There "In the Book." For example, what were the names of James's aunts in *James and the Giant Peach* (Dahl, 1961)? The answer (Aunt Sponge and Aunt Spiker) is in the book; you can even point to it. Think and Search questions are also in the book, but the answers need to be pulled together from different parts of the book. For example, name the places to which James and the peach traveled: this is a Think and Search question because the answer, although in the book, is located in multiple chapters.

Boys tend to focus on facts when reading; so, it is especially worthwhile for them to practice answering "In My Head" questions, which entail either (1) Author and Me or (2) On My Own answers. Author and Me questions invite students to consider the story as well as the author's message and then integrate these with their own life experiences and interpretations to answer. One example might be: How would you face the challenge of living in a giant peach? To answer that question, students would both need to know something about living in a peach but also consider what they think would be challenging about living in a peach.

Students would not necessarily have to have read the book to answer an On My Own question since, in answering, they rely only on their own experiences and views. One example would be: What might happen if "the biggest bomb in the history of the world was hovering over" (Dahl, 1961, p. 108) the city in which you lived? Clearly this question can be answered without having read about the peach floating over New York City.

The QAR approach is helpful to boys because it better enables them to understand where to find the answer to a certain type of question (Gunning, 2008). Boys also should understand that there is a connection between the question type and its answer (Schirmer, 2010). Some questions are literal, but some are inferential and require higher-level thinking.

Think-Alouds

Thinking aloud (Davey, 1983) is a strategy that improves comprehension by verbalizing one's internal thinking, thus making more apparent the processes that naturally occur during reading. In other words, thinking aloud forces students to think while reading. Consciously using that inner voice while reading helps boys to monitor their use of such other strategies as predicting, imaging, connecting, and clearing up confusion. Although it is important for teachers to model any new strategy, it is vital that they model think-alouds and allow sufficient time for students to practice the strategy often in the classroom.

Teachers should plan their think-aloud modeling session well ahead of time to ensure a proper presentation. The following sample think-aloud, from Humphrey's *Pompeii: Nightmare at Midnight* (1996, p. 29), focuses on the events immediately after Mount Vesuvius erupted a second time, releasing deadly gasses and tons of ash that buried the inhabitants of Pompeii:

> TEXT: A woman died clutching her jewels.
>
> TEACHER: She must have been trying to escape if she had her valuables. She might have been from the part of town where the wealthy lived. Maybe the jewels were excavated and are now displayed in a museum or at the site of Pompeii.
>
> TEXT: A slave died draped over plates he had dropped.
>
> TEACHER: I wonder if this was the slave of the woman with the jewels. He must have been working as the ground was shaking. Maybe the plates dropped because the ground shook! He must have been terrified.
>
> TEXT: A man begging outside the city gate died with his sack.
>
> TEACHER: This man was *outside* the gate with a sack. I wonder what he had in his sack. I guess they were *his* valuables. He could have been trying to get away

from the destruction in the town. This makes me think of deadly fumes and fires. Even now it isn't always the flames that kill people, but many times it is the fumes from toxic materials. The fumes killed many in Pompeii. Maybe more people could have escaped had it not been for the deadly gasses released into the air.

TEXT: At least 2,000 people were killed and buried by the ashes covering Pompeii.

TEACHER: Two thousand people! That is a little more than the number of people that died in Hurricane Katrina and about the same number of students in our district's high schools and middle schools combined. If 2,000 people were killed and buried in Pompeii, I wonder how many more died in Herculaneum.

After the teacher's modeling of the method, students work with partners, alternately reading the next section of text and practicing the think-aloud. To ensure boys' active engagement, the teacher made sure the topic was interesting and motivating, the text included dramatic photos and clear graphics, background information about Pompeii and volcanoes was provided, and same-gender partners worked together. To ensure success and automaticity over time, the think-aloud strategy was repeatedly modeled, students were coached, and the strategy was practiced over a period of weeks.

Smith and Wilhelm (2006) have suggested other types of thinking aloud for their male students. These include (1) free-response think-alouds, in which students write as they read; (2) cued think-alouds, wherein students respond to a specific visual or written cue; and (3) visual think-alouds, in which drawings represent the text or students' connections to the reading (pp. 107–108).

GETTING TO THE CONTENT

Textbooks are the major tool for teaching in the content areas. However, textbooks are relatively dry reading and the content occasionally confusing or misleading. Since textbooks may attract little interest from boys (and girls for that matter), fortunately there are alternative ways to help learn the content. First, many textbooks have allied websites where students can view much the same materials and sometimes even more, including related photos, videos, and hypermedia links. Second, reading everything from picture books to professional books on the same topic helps to stoke students' interest and understanding of the topics covered in the textbooks. For example, first graders might be studying their local neighborhoods in social studies. To supplement the textbook's information, fiction and nonfiction sources providing further background knowledge—in addition to books on the history, famous people, and events of the wider community—should be made available in a special section of the classroom library.

Videos, podcasts, blogs, interviews, and software also help boys understand content. At *pbskids.org/rogers/buildANeighborhood.html*, first graders can build their own neighborhood; at *www.nationalgeographic.com/podcasts,* students can learn about animals from their community as well as around the world; and at *www.studentsoftheworld.info/sites/pages.php,* students can read blogs about communities in different countries. Another significant resource that can provide useful images that help boys learn content is YouTube. Performing an online search of the name of your own town might reveal a number of interesting videos—like the one featuring a train cutting through the village of Glenview, Illinois, on a winter morning (available at *www.youtube.com/watch?v=h5HHFibEYhw&NR=1*)!

To make more sense of the content, boys can be encouraged to create and use such visual aids as photos, graphs, outlines, diagrams, charts, and the like. These graphic organizers help clarify informational relationships and structure content so that it is easier to learn (Tate, 2003). Boys can create and use their own graphic organizers when they are provided with oversized paper, rulers, and drawing pencils, which is generally better than having to use an organizer copied onto an 8" x 11" sheet of paper. When using a graphic organizer for the first time, boys are most successful when they are able to copy a model.

One class assignment was to compare and contrast a hurricane and a tornado by using a Venn diagram. Venn diagrams had been modeled in past lessons; so, the students were familiar with the form and the process. The same-gender partners drew two large intersecting circles traced onto unruled chart paper and then filled in the similarities and differences between tornados and hurricanes by using both words and pictures. This exercise was successful with boys because they were (1) using sufficiently large paper to accommodate any issues with handwriting in small spaces; (2) organizing knowledge to assist in their understanding; (3) paying attention to the details of the graphic organizer; (4) able to use pictures; (5) able to replicate the process with practice; and (6) able to complete the task entirely.

The Venn diagram assignment was also successful because of the partner work. Boys work well when they are able to talk, be active, and yet include a bit of play (Fletcher, 2006). Alex, a middle school science teacher, observes this dynamic unfolding in his classes every day:

> "I often see that boys working in same-gender groups have less of the pressure to 'perform'—especially for their female peers. In this sense, boys working among themselves often show me deeper knowledge and collaborative skills without having to worry about social stigmas sometimes associated with being studious. I find that I see the most critical thinking and growth with boys when they challenge each other and themselves for the betterment of their group."

Alex enthusiastically talks about how well his male students work together. Alex is a fairly new teacher, but he clearly understands how to reach boys. He understands literacy and how boys "work" with content, both as a hands-on activity and, as much as possible, as an extension of what they enjoy (Fletcher, 2006; Newkirk, 2002).

DIGITAL LITERACIES AND BOYS

The lives of boys have changed radically during the past decade. Boys as young as three own video systems and handheld Internet devices, and they play network and browser-based games with friends online. They don't necessarily need to go out to socialize; they can keep in touch with friends through texting, Facebook, and Twitter. A study by the Kaiser Family Foundation (2010) found that in general those between the ages of 8 and 18 spend an average of 7 hours and 38 minutes a day involved in what they call "entertainment media." The heaviest media users were boys between the ages of 11 and 14, and many who reported heavy use also reported lower grades in school.

Because they are so heavily immersed in it, contemporary school-age children are native users of the digital language needed to effectively interface with today's electronic and digital literacies (Zambo & Brozo, 2009). They are also the best teachers of electronic and digital literacies. Boys in particular seem to be able to figure out these new media without parents' or teachers' assistance. When asked how he learned to use his new video game system, Will explained, "I just jumped into it. I had a little experience playing at a friend's house; so, when I got mine, I just kept trying things until something worked." Will didn't use the manual, and he laughed when asked if his parents had helped him get familiar with the games. "My parents read the manual, but that was only to set the system up. They still don't really know how to use it."

The skills boys have with electronic and other high-tech media will indeed be significant in shaping their future—but so will literacy. The two can be combined to deepen the learning and knowledge that arise from reading and writing. Gauthier et al. (2006–2007) found that shared web spaces like various wiki links and Google Docs were tools that boys found to be highly accessible and easy to use. Google Docs and wikis allow users to collaboratively compose, revise, edit, and add hyperlinks to content while using any web browser (*www.docs.google.com*; *www.wiki.org*). Using these links, a research paper could be completed by a group of boys over the Internet without ever having to physically get together.

In the Gauthier et al. study (2006–2007), boys had to work in groups of twos and threes on either long-term science projects or American History textbook chapter outlines. Assignments were distributed so that each individual group member had to contribute equally to the assignment's completion. The groups were able track their efforts, and the teachers were able to monitor their progress while including their own reflections and comments right on the web document.

The completed assignments were found to include more data and ideas of a higher quality when these web-based methods were employed. Approximately three-fourths of the boys said that they would gladly use shared web spaces again for group work. They noted that the web spaces were easy to use and that they were able to be well organized without having to worry about losing their materials. They especially liked being able to work on the collaborative web space at any time and not having to meet directly with their partners in order to complete their assignments. They noted that the web space provided a better collaborative arrangement than having to email documents back and forth.

IMPLEMENTING KEY IDEAS

Literacy leaders realize that, as readers, boys have special or even unique needs when it comes to literacy. In this chapter we have reviewed these unique needs and recommend a few key ways to support boys in literacy:

- Discover the areas of interest for all students—but especially for boys.
- Have a variety of engaging reading genres available for boys' appraisal and selection.
- Make multiple book recommendations in diverse genres readily available.
- Implement SSR to encourage a love of reading.
- Urge both parents, especially fathers, to read more.
- Teach boys engaging comprehension strategies to bolster their understanding.
- Help boys contend better with textbook content by a variety of means.
- Promote digital literacy technology to engage boys further in literacy activities.

CONCLUDING THOUGHTS

Literacy leaders are committed to providing all students with the tools to be able to read and write, but the gender gap still needs to narrow. On a positive note, the National Endowment for the Arts (2009) study found that after years of decrease, the literature reading for 18- to 24-year-olds in general increased 21 percent between 2002 and 2008 and that the literature reading for males increased at an 11 percent rate during the same years. It is time to implement what is known about the special literacy needs of boys and commit to supporting boy readers. Embracing and celebrating boys and literacy just makes good sense.

CHAPTER FIVE

Literacy Leadership in Middle School
Building a Community of Book Lovers

> Good teachers possess a capacity of connectedness. They are
> able to weave a complex web of connections among themselves,
> their subjects, and their students so that students can learn to
> weave a world for themselves.
> —PARKER PALMER, *The Courage to Teach*

- -

It is a warm, sunny spring day and during the period between classes at Glen Bend
Middle School as music plays quietly throughout the school. Tunes selected by teachers
and students fill the rooms and halls as students move quickly from one classroom to
another.

In Mrs. Best and Mrs. Long's three-period literacy class, students who have been
identified as less able readers remain in the same classroom, where Mrs. Best announces,
"It is chatting time." Teachers and students mingle, use the restroom, converse, and
enjoy a few minutes of downtime before the next period officially begins. After the bell
rings, the students settle naturally into three literacy-focused groups, one group working
with Mrs. Long, another with Mrs. Best, and the remaining students working individually at their computers.

Mrs. Best sits in her chair in this cozy room with a group of six students. She begins
her lesson with a question.

MRS. BEST: Who has ever been deprived of something in their life?

SAMMI: The one time I got into trouble was because I was deprived of my privileges
because I was being bad in school.

SALLY: I was deprived because I gave my cousin something of mine and never got
it back.

All six students in turn expressively share their experiences of being deprived. In
this literature discussion, the conversation is authentic, with the participants expressing

ideas and opinions while listening and learning from one another. Having shared personal experiences that they will use to relate to the story, the students are ready to read a passage from *Bud, Not Buddy* (Curtis, 1999). This story is about a 10-year-old boy named Bud Caldwell who has run away from an impersonal orphanage and a cruel foster home to search for his birth father. To help establish the purposes for the reading and to generate further discussion, Mrs. Best prepared an anticipation guide that mentions some of the characters and situations that appear in the passage to be read (see Figure 5.1). Because Mrs. Best hooked the students with a thought-provoking introductory question, a guide to matters to anticipate in the reading, and a subsequent discussion, the members of the group were more fully engaged in the reading.

BOTH TEACHERS AND STUDENTS MAY FACILITATE ENJOYMENT OF BOOKS

It is axiomatic that in order to become a good reader one must take time to read frequently. But a supervising adult is not always the one who should motivate students to love reading. Students themselves not only can facilitate the love of reading but also can

Name: _____

Date: _____

Book title: *Bud, Not Buddy*

BEFORE: MARK **A** OR **D**
Read the sentences below before you read the passage. Mark your predictions as *A* if you agree that the sentence correctly predicts what will happen or *D* if you disagree and do not believe the sentence correctly predicts what will happen.

AFTER: MARK **T** OR **F**
Read the sentences again after you read the passage. Mark *T* if the sentence is true and *F* if the sentence is false.

1. _____   After escaping from the shed, Bud sneaks into the basement of the library for the night. _____

2. _____   Bud has one picture of his mom that is covered with filth. _____

3. _____   Bud is named after a flower bud. _____

4. _____   The Amoses fumbled through Bud's suitcase and stole some items from it. _____

5. _____   Bud does not want to go to the mission for breakfast. _____

FIGURE 5.1. Anticipation guide for literature exploration.

teach their peers skills related to reading improvement (Moskal & Blachowicz, 2006). In any learning community some readers are less able than others, but all students can cheer one another on and learn from one another as they read, listen, discuss, and write.

As the chief decision makers within the literacy curriculum, teachers play a vital role in creating a community of book lovers. Darling-Hammond (2009) blogs: "The single most important determinant of what students learn is what their teachers know. Teacher qualifications, knowledge, and skills make more difference for a student learning than any other single factor." Teachers model reading behaviors and show students how to work both alone and in partnership with others. They often step back from "teaching" to become facilitators and good listeners. They then scaffold, or coach, their students to do the same.

This chapter presents a class community of less able readers, including English language learners (ELLs), who nonetheless develop a love of books. They continually learn to work together and use strategies to develop their reading and writing skills, facilitated by the hard work of their teachers, who believe that students should be responsible for their own learning and that motivation is a major factor in success (Roller & Fielding, 1998). The teachers are interested in the students' ideas, they strive to be fair, and they share in the learning (Johnston & Nichols, 1995; Sergiovanni, 1994).

Mrs. Long and Mrs. Best reveal how they teach and facilitate literacy learning to ensure that their students come to love reading. After providing an overview of the three-block literacy plan, we focus in this chapter on how to implement collaboration, engagement, and motivational techniques, as well as questioning strategies and group learning. Next, we extend the community of book lovers to include senior citizens. At the end of the chapter we offer additional implementation ideas.

OVERVIEW OF THE THREE-BLOCK LITERACY PLAN

Glen Bend Middle School, located in a suburb of Chicago, serves some 700 students in the sixth through eighth grades. The students' parents are highly supportive and closely involved in the day-to-day functioning of the school. Special-needs programs include early childhood, gifted education, learning disabilities resources, literacy, speech and language, and english as a second language. The average class size ranges from 21 to 25 students.

Mrs. Long is a reading specialist at Glen Bend Middle School; Mrs. Best is a special educator and reading specialist in the district. Several years ago Mrs. Best and Mrs. Long submitted proposals to the school board to service students who did not fit into the IEP category but who were assessed to be struggling readers or transitional English learners. The proposal recommended a program for students to learn across a three-period block of time to develop and strengthen literacy strategies and skills and, in a separate program, to read assigned materials in the traditional content areas. Mrs. Long lamented that "struggling readers need to do a lot more informational text reading and receive appropriate explicit instruction focused on developing thoughtful, critical literacy skills." The school board approved both programs for the following school year.

Assessment

AIMSweb testing (Pearson Psych Corp., 2010) and Illinois State Achievement Test (ISAT; *www.isbe.state.il.us/assessment/ISAT.htm*) scores are used at the beginning of the year to determine student eligibility for the three-block literacy class. Generally, Mrs. Best and Mrs. Long together enlist between 16 and 20 students each year, assessing their progress throughout the academic year by means of AIMSweb testing.

Organization of the Three Blocks

The three-period block literacy program is described in Figure 5.2. Mrs. Long and Mrs. Best work with some 20 sixth graders in a three-block literacy class every day. The teachers and students work together shoulder-to-shoulder in collaborative small groups. The students internalize learning as a dynamic process in this closely knit community of learners characterized by trusting relationships. The clear guidelines and expectations that were established from the beginning of the school year are evident in this dynamic learning community.

The three-period block literacy schedule is 2½ hours long, divided into the three instructional sessions between 11:15 A.M. and 1:30 P.M.

- 11:15–11:50   Group A—Mrs. Long; Group B—Mrs. Best; Group C—computers
- 12:00–12:45   Group B—Mrs. Long; Group C—Mrs. Best; Group A—computers
- 12:55–1:30   Group C—Mrs. Long; Group A—Mrs. Best; Group B—computers

The system of rotation enables all the students to participate in discussing literature, work on reading skills development, and practice with computers. The exact membership of the groups changes daily, depending upon the particular skill and strategy being taught that day.

Mrs. Long and Mrs. Best use the Read 180 (Scholastic, n.d.) multimedia technology program, both on an individual basis and as supplemental materials in the classroom. The program, designed by researchers at Vanderbilt University, and featuring interactive CDs with full-motion video, provides interactive readings adjusted to students' assessed reading level as well as spelling and word study materials.

A Collegial and Safe Environment

Mrs. Long and Mrs. Best allow for movement throughout the 2½-hour-time period by giving students the 5 minutes they would normally use to move between classes plus

DESCRIPTION

This class is designed to help students whose reading levels do not qualify them for the Reading Lab but who are reading below class expectations; are transitioning out of English language learner (ELL), English language bridging (ELB), or Reading Lab; are recently dismissed ELLs; or are struggling with content-area reading. Currently students who are reading beyond the level of Reading Lab and many ELLs struggle in social studies and science classes owing in part to trouble with reading required texts and tests. Many of these students also find novel-length reading within their literacy classes to be difficult as a result of the large volume of independent reading and the varying levels of the books. Students are given instruction in strategies to use in their classes, support with class materials, and additional curriculum-relevant readings in parallel texts. The focus is on helping students deal with the large volume of informational texts they will be confronted with for the rest of their lives. Instruction is delivered through the application of research-based best practices in reading instruction, including vocabulary development; pre-, during, and postreading strategies; responses to reading materials; and critical literacy.

GOAL

The goal of the program is to help students read at or above grade-level expectations and be successful readers in their classes. As students reach this goal, they will be moved out of the program.

STUDENT SELECTION

Students will be selected based on standardized, formal, and informal assessments and scores in addition to teacher recommendations.

STAFFING

Because the program is designed to support transitional ELLs and striving readers, it will be taught by a reading specialist and ELL instructor. Keeping the teacher–student ratio low allows for more individualized instruction and accelerated transition time.

MATERIALS

Social studies and science textbooks and parallel texts (when needed) will be used for strategy instruction and practice. Additional nonfiction materials for strategy instruction are also used.

FIGURE 5.2. Mrs. Long's Content-Area Reading Strategies (CARS) program.

an extra 5 minutes to talk, take bathroom breaks, and relax between the group sessions. Lively discussions characterize this time period as students exchange greetings and pleasantries. Caring conversations between teachers and students also contribute to the "safe" environment deliberately cultivated by the teachers, one in which students are free to express their ideas candidly without fear of harsh judgment or intimidation.

Reading with Others

Another aspect of this exemplary program is how its activities are integrated with the wider community through the participation of senior citizens from a local assisted-living facility, The Meadows. Twice a month between 16–20 seniors from the residential complex visit Mrs. Long and Mrs. Best's classes for a shared reading session with their students.

A COMMUNITY OF BOOK LOVERS

Fostering Supportive Relationships

Developing a well-established community of learners is important to any educational environment (Peterson, 1992). At Glen Bend Middle School, Mrs. Long and Mrs. Best create a reading environment that emphasizes positive and supportive teacher–student and student–student relationships. The teachers' philosophy emphasizes the importance of the students' emotions and feelings, and their interpersonal skills convey the message that every student is highly valued. The relationships fostered by the teachers are consistent with Carney's (1999) definition of a community of learners as "a place where student learners are made to feel that their prior knowledge, the knowledge that they are acquiring, and the skills they are learning in order to acquire future knowledge are all tied together" (p. 53). This is a vibrant, active, supportive community of learners where the relationships that are sown and nourished ultimately lead to mutual collaboration and success.

In the context of these collaborative and supportive relationships, students arriving daily at Mrs. Long and Mrs. Best's classroom door and spend the first few minutes talking to one another about various aspects of their prospective day. They use this informal social interaction to reconnect with their peers and find out what is new before beginning to work, enabling them to transition into the three-period block where, once personal connections have been made, the focus shifts to literacy concerns.

Relationships thrive when teachers really know their students well and students also know one another well. There is shared sense of active listening as everyone contributes to reading discussions and shares connections to books. Because of this positive atmosphere, students are not afraid to speak up and voice their unvarnished opinions. They know their contribution is valuable and important to the group's collective understanding. Respectful relationships that support and encourage everyone's active participation facilitate the learning process.

Ideally, there is also a respectful relationship between students and teachers that goes beyond learning. One afternoon when the students arrived in the classroom, they immediately noticed a "funny" smell in the room that caused a bit of consternation and puzzlement. Mrs. Best immediately set the students at ease, explaining the class immediately before had read a story in which the main character ate eggs with sauce, and the students had spontaneously decided to cook and eat the same dish, leaving behind the unusual smell. This timely explanation was much appreciated by all, and the students then went about the business of the daily activities together. On another day, the students came into the room and it rapidly became quite noisy with many conversations. All it took was a firm "We need to get going … " by Mrs. Best to quiet the room instantly, as students quickly settled in and were ready to listen.

Although Eisner (2002) states that supportive and caring conversations are the rarest feature of classroom life, they are not rare in the three-block literacy class. Concrete strategies to nurture relationships such as "small talk" at the beginning of class, sharing stories and feelings, and discuss the readings both during and after class have a sub-stantial impact on learning and the values that build a community of learners (Nevin, Thousand, & Villa, 1994; Peterson, 1992).

An Engaging and Motivating Reading Curriculum

Materials

Allington (2008) writes that students' reading success could be enhanced by redesign-ing lessons to provide books that the students would actually *enjoy* reading. Teachers should take the time to maximize book choices for students that are appropriate, inter-esting, and at the right reading level (whether instructional or recreational in emphasis) for small-group and whole-class literature discussions. Time spent in selecting the best books for students to read is a worthwhile endeavor that benefits all learners.

The books ultimately selected for inclusion shold reflect students' interests. Sur-veys and self-reports give students the opportunity to share their interests so that teach-ers and librarians can be well informed about their diverse preferences. When reading selections touch on areas of interest, struggling readers are more likely to engage with the materials and to push themselves even when the reading is at a challenging level.

Teachers can also facilitate a love of books by advocating the widest possible offer-ing of diverse reading materials. In that way, students never feel restrained, and because they are given meaningful choices students feel respected and responsible, thus ensur-ing greater motivation on their part and a willingness to engage in reading for sheer enjoyment.

Book Discussion Groups

Successfully forming a community of book lovers also has its roots in students' par-ticipation in book discussion groups, which also helps to motivate reading. Through the groups, students participate in small- and whole-group discussions that demonstrate, even highlight, the diversity of their peers' opinions. Some researchers suggest that the informal, low-stakes atmosphere of conversation about books has a positive effect on students' sense of competence as readers (e.g., Blum, Lipsett, & Yocum, 2002), also increasing their confidence in their own ideas (Katz & Kirby, 2001–2002; Kong & Fitch, 2002–2003).

Discussions also allow students to communicate by using "kid-talk" (Rogoff, 1990), in the words of one teacher. "They seem to have their own language. They are able to express their thoughts and ideas to each other in a way that I can't. I use teacher language and kids explain in kids' language" (Antil, Jenkins, Wayne, & Vadasy, 1998, p. 424).

The students in Mrs. Long and Mrs. Best's class talk a lot, but it is useful and pur-poseful talk that helps them to clarify their ideas, to ask better questions, and to sum-marize and synthesize ideas more easily. By reading and talking to others about books, students come to think about the books in ways that are different than when they read alone (Vygotsky, 1978). This reading and mutual discussion together afford the opportunity for readers to inquire with others, listen to others' opinions, and create deeper understanding within themselves (Langer, 1992). Langer and Flihan (2000) state that the social activity generated within any small group helps all participants experience a deeper understanding of the matter discussed.

Periodically, students work on book reports together in book discussion groups (see Figure 5.3 for a sample book report form). One example is when groups read books on famous people. Mrs. Best and Mrs. Long scaffold their students' thinking by asking the following questions:

- "Why do you think the author chose to write about this person?"
- "How do the illustrations help you understand the story?"
- "Which illustration does your group like best and why?"

By working as a group, students are able to pool their collective knowledge, reread passages from the book to clarify any confusion, extend their thinking in diverse directions, and deepen their understanding as they discuss the book with one another. These authentic reading experiences enable the students to accomplish the learning goals that were developed for the lesson.

Learning from Exemplary Questioning Strategies

Questioning has always been an important aspect of teaching and fundamental to outstanding pedagogy (Frazee & Rudnitski, 1995; Klein, Peterson, & Simington, 1991; Nunan & Lamb, 1996). Effective questioning by the teacher is believed to focus students' attention on several aspects of a lesson, namely, understanding its content, arousing students' curiosity, stimulating their imagination, and increasing their motives to learn. When done skillfully, questioning elevates students' level of thinking (Muth & Alvermann, 1992; Orlich, Harder, Callahan, Kauchak, & Gibson, 1994; Ornstein, 1995). Devising and posing good questions also helps teachers to assess their students' learning and to revise and modify the lessons as needed. Despite the fact that good questioning improves learning, studies show that exemplary questioning is rarely carried out successfully in teaching.

Both Mrs. Long and Mrs. Best, as expert teachers, use exemplary questioning strategies when working in small groups or the whole class. Both teachers pose more "open" questions (i.e., where multiple or free-form responses are required) and value good thinking over the "correct" answer. Both teachers have a thorough understanding of how children learn, and they are skilled in implementing questioning strategies throughout their teaching block.

Mrs. Best and Mrs. Long use questions often in their teaching. They ask questions at the beginning of the small-group discussions to activate students' prior knowledge

COOPERATIVE GROUP BOOK REPORT

Group Members: _____

_____

Date: _____

Title of the Biography: _____

_____

Author(s): _____ Illustrator(s): _____

Who is your book about?

_____

_____

Why do you think the author chose to write about this person?

_____

_____

How do the illustrations help you to understand the story?

_____

_____

Which illustration does your group like best and why? Page _____

_____

_____

We did not understand/know the following words:

Page   Word   Page   Word

FIGURE 5.3. Sample of a cooperative group book report.

before reading the selections (e.g., "What is the story about so far?" "Have you ever had a similar experience?). They also use followup questions to encourage students to elaborate on their initial answer ("How do you know?" "Tell me more." "Can you explain?"). They readily accept more than one answer to any question in a discussion. Additionally they encourage students to ask questions of one another.

Both Mrs. Long and Mrs. Best value the students' thoughts and ideas in this learner-centered environment. The students pose questions to their teacher and classmates to express and share ideas and to show they are participating actively while developing their thinking skills and reading skills (Burden & Byrd, 1994; Orlich et al., 1994).

Ensuring Comprehension

One afternoon, Mrs. Long's group of students was reading the Scholastic version of *Dr. Jekyll and Mr. Hyde* by Robert Louis Stevenson (1886/2001) and practicing lines from a script for an upcoming readers' theater version of the story. Mrs. Long invited all six members of the group to read their script parts aloud. This was not a typical round-robin reading, however. The students had had an opportunity to practice their part before the day's lesson; so, they were comfortable with the read-aloud portion of the lesson (Moskal & Blachowicz, 2006). All group members listened to their classmates intently, silently cheering one another on to read successfully. They were serious and committed to their earlier class discussion about the story and knew how to read the parts with expression.

After practicing their script lines, the students were invited to watch a 2-minute film clip on *Dr. Jekyll and Mr. Hyde* via a YouTube clip (*www.youtube.com/watch?v=ho8-vK0L1_8*). This was a clip from the original black-and-white version of the story. This clip mesmerized all the students. Mrs. Long asked the students questions about the similarities and differences between the clip and the passage in the book, and a lively discussion ensued. The students asked clarifying questions seeking to compare the clip to the story they had read. The culminating activity was the readers' theater 40-minute performance by the students.

Making Connections to Real Life Experiences

The students in Mrs. Best and Mrs. Long's class are consistently encouraged during the cooperative literacy groups to make connections between the literature they read and their own real-life experiences. Harste, Woodward, and Burke (1986) define learning as the process of making connections and searching for patterns that connect to make sense of the world. The students in Mrs. Best and Mrs. Long's class are given ample opportunities to make such connections to their real-life experiences.

Poetry

To begin the three-period block literacy class one day, there was a poetry reading in celebration of poetry month. Mrs. Long selected and read a poem titled "Sunday Night Meltdown" from the book *Swimming Upstream: Middle School Poems* by Kristine O'Connell George (2002). George's wonderful book of poems chronicles the trials and tribulations of middle school life.

Mrs. Long asked, "Why do you think the book is called *Swimming Upstream?* and after a thoughtful discussion she modeled a think-aloud that made connections to the students' experiences in elementary school as compared to their first days of middle school. She asked many questions to encourage the students to think aloud about how they felt that first day of sixth grade, leaving grade school for middle school—for example:

- "How hard was it to locate your locker?"
- "How difficult was it to find your homeroom?"
- "Put yourself in the place again of just starting middle school."

Students continued to think aloud and make connections about the beginning of the school year and how it was like swimming upstream. Next, Mrs. Long read the poem aloud again, followed by a choral reading by the students.

Mrs. Best and Mrs. Long created a couple of worksheets to help students develop their skills in understanding poetry by making their own personal connections to it (see Figures 5.4 and 5.5). In this way, students were taught to pay attention to the details of the poems to help them connect to the poet's meaning and to enable them to enjoy the class poetry readings all the more.

A Lesson on Child Labor

One afternoon Mrs. Best began a lesson by asking "Whom do you think made some of the shirts, shoes, and basketballs you own?" The dialogue that followed both drew from and expanded the students' background knowledge while showing that they were thinking in earnest about how children their own age or younger had to work long hours in foreign sweatshops.

The students then read a short article from *Time for Kids* magazine documenting the employment of young children in other countries who work in harsh conditions. Mrs. Best showed a video clip that illustrated how these children work in factories located in other countries to produce a lot of the clothes and sports equipment that children in the United States use. All the students in the class were engaged in this thought-provoking lesson. The lesson made them think about their own lives and connect to what it would be like to work full-time in the factories depicted in the *Time for Kids* article.

1. Choose a poem you like that is at least six lines long, but not too long to memorize. The title of the poem I choose is: _____

_____

2. Practice reading the poem out loud. Make sure you are pronouncing all the words correctly. Ask for help if you need it.

   WORDS I NEED TO LEARN: _____

_____

_____

_____

_____

_____

3. Read the poem many times. Focus on FLUENCY (appropriate pace, word accuracy, smoothness, phrasing, and expression).

4. Practice reading the poem again with good voice volume, direct eye contact, and appropriate gestures.

5. Read the poem to a friend or small group of people. Ask them to share what you did well, and write below what you still need to practice.

   I STILL NEED TO PRACTICE: _____

_____

_____

_____

**On _____ you will present your poem to the class for a grade. You cannot read it; it will need to be memorized!

   You will be graded on word accuracy, eye contact, expression, voice volume, and all aspects of fluency. Your recitation should demonstrate that you understand the poem.

FIGURE 5.4. Poetry presentation.

Name: _____

Date: _____

Today I read (list the title of the poetry book): _____

_____

One interesting poem was titled: _____

_____

In my opinion, it was about: _____

_____

_____

_____

My favorite line was: _____

_____

_____

I chose this line because: _____

_____

_____

_____

_____

The author really does a good job of: _____

_____

_____

_____

_____

FIGURE 5.5. Poetry investigation.

Using Reading Strategies Independently

"Will you share what you know about the strategy we practiced yesterday?" Mrs. Long and Mrs. Best often ask, adding, "You need to think about using the strategy—how it can help and when it can help during a time when you are reading alone." The focus is properly on helping the students become independent and actively employ the strategies they are learning to monitor their reading appropriately. Students who believe in their own ability to comprehend texts and construct meaning are far more likely to complete assignments successfully (Schunk & Zimmerman, 1997). By using reading strategies independently, the students are learning to rely on their own ability to read and comprehend.

In Mrs. Long and Mrs. Best's classroom, students are helped to internalize reading strategies for accomplishing the task of reading independently. Brownell (2000) asserts that strategy instruction should be well integrated into the teacher's ongoing lessons. This "integration" occurs during the three-period block literacy class. The focus is not on the answer but on *how to get* the answer and the process of learning.

When small groups are working properly, the students often remind one another about strategy use, saying, "Go back and reread the word—let's see if we can find the meaning," or "Try to remember the name of the main character." Under these circumstances the students are learning the importance of being a "Real Reader" (see Figure 5.6) and are using fix-up strategies constantly as they read. Often struggling readers just keep going when reading (McCray, Vaughn & Neal, 2001, p. 22) and don't even have a clue that they made a mistake. However, the struggling readers in Mrs. Long and Mrs. Best's classroom learn to self-monitor to make sure that what they read makes sense to them as they go.

Cooperative Learners

Mrs. Long and Mrs. Best's rotation schedule allows ample opportunities for them to present small cooperative group lessons that enhance learning. Johnson, Johnson, and Holubec (1993) describe cooperative learning as "the instructional use of small groups so that students work together to maximize their own and each other's learning" (p. 6). In Mrs. Best and Mrs. Long's class, these small cooperative learning groups facilitate academic learning.

The students in their class participate fully and actively for the entire three-period block of instruction. Learning in small groups enables the students to listen closely and respond respectfully to their peers as well as strive to get along with all their classmates. In cooperative learning groups, students have many opportunities to clarify their thinking, interpret complex instructions, explain their ideas, give feedback and instructions, scaffold their problem-solving efforts, and provide encouragement. These are skills that benefit struggling learners and help them succeed. The cooperative grouping helps students to develop social skills that are readily evident and a valuable by-product of the instructional tools they use in this well-organized classroom.

The benefits of working together as a cooperative community are many. Students understand that their membership in a learning group means that they either succeed

Are you a REAL READER or a FAKE READER?

FAKE READER	REAL READER
◆ Fake Reader stares at the pages.	★ Real Reader thinks about what was read.
◆ Fake Reader turns the pages too quickly.	★ Real Reader is focused on the text.
◆ Fake Reader doesn't know anything about the story.	★ Real Reader can retell the story at the end.
◆ Fake Reader talks to friends while reading until the teacher looks at him or her and then says "Oh yeah" and turns the pages.	★ Real Reader scores above 80% on quizzes.
	★ Real Reader can be heard when reading aloud.
◆ Fake Reader doesn't say the correct words.	★ Real Reader asks for help when needed.
◆ Fake Reader hides behind a big book.	★ Real Reader writes about the story.
◆ Fake Reader scores below 60% on quizzes.	★ Real Reader focuses and concentrates deeply.
◆ Fake Reader lies about reading.	★ Real Reader can answer questions at the end of a chapter.
◆ Fake Reader avoids answering questions about the book by trying to change the subject, like "Can I go to the bathroom?"	★ Real Reader responds specifically.
◆ Fake Reader gets caught skipping parts.	★ Real Reader finishes reading in a timely manner.
◆ Fake Reader only looks at the pictures and doesn't read the text and captions.	
◆ Fake Reader takes too long to read one page.	
◆ Fake Reader cannot summarize what was just read.	

FIGURE 5.6. Sample of a Real Reader handout.

or fail together (Deutsch, 1962). Students help one another learn and encourage each individual member's success. More importantly, individuals in the group understand that they are accountable to one another and to the group.

EXTENDING THE COMMUNITY TO INCLUDE BOOK LOVERS AT THE MEADOWS

Once 2 two weeks, the students in Mrs. Long and Mrs. Best's class have visitors from a local assisted-living residence, The Meadows. The Meadows's residents are bused to the school to spend one literacy period reading with their younger buddies. The students look forward to this day with great anticipation and enjoy the time spent reading together. When Mrs. Best and Mrs. Long originally approached The Meadows Senior Community with the idea of becoming reading buddies to their class of sixth-grade struggling readers, the seniors were enthusiastic about helping the students. The seniors were paired up with students in the class and served as regular "reading buddies" throughout the year.

One day in March, Darren raised his hand to volunteer to greet the senior visitors and walk them from the main office to the classroom. While Darren was out of the room, Mrs. Best and Mrs. Long asked the students to take out the Valentine's Day cards they made for their visitors. They had kept the cards since the seniors were unable to come in mid-February, owing to illness. Darren walked the visitors from the main office back to the classroom.

Upon entering the classroom, the seniors met with their partner students, who then handed them their Valentine's Day cards. After thanks, much affection, and many kisses, the reading began. Darren's senior friend sat close to him, and the pair began to read. The reading selections on that day focused on the subject of natural disasters. The seniors and students read selections that the students had chosen on the topic, and it was not easy reading! For 45 minutes the students and their senior friends were actively involved in the act of reading, supporting one another to make sense of the challenging text.

Bringing older people and schoolchildren together creates a bond between the two groups and rewards for both that surpass the literacy experience (Sellars, 1998). This special synergy was very clear the day Ayn visited Mrs. Best and Mrs. Long's class—clearly, everyone was benefiting from the shared reading time. While senior volunteers can be recruited from a variety of places, Mrs. Best and Mrs. Long were fortunate to have an assisted-living community close to the school with seniors who were happy to be part of their learning community.

A COMMUNITY OF BOOK LOVERS ARE PREPARED FOR SEVENTH GRADE

Mrs. Long reported that 15 of the 20 sixth-grade students from the class described in this chapter successfully integrated into the regular seventh-grade literacy classes but still received some additional literacy support. Three students continued in the seventh grade with no support, and two of the students entered into the self-contained special education class. All the students continue to be closely monitored to ensure learning and success, but their experiences in the three-block literacy class prepared them for implementing literacy skills and positive learning behaviors across all their classes.

WHY THE THREE-BLOCK LITERACY CLASS WORKED FOR STRUGGLING SIXTH-GRADE READERS

Allington (2001) noted that numerous studies have cited teacher knowledge and skill as significant factors in successfully teaching those who struggle in attaining proficient reading skills. Mrs. Best and Mrs. Long were not only reading and educational specialists but also teachers knowledgeable about classroom management practices that encouraged self-esteem, risk taking, and self-regulation. They continued their own education through graduate coursework and professional development training to ensure that they could provide exemplary learning experiences for their students.

The two taught sufficiently well that their students were arguably in Vygotsky's (1978) zone of proximal development (ZPD), where the student—when scaffolded by those more knowledgeable—can make rapid progress. ZPD is defined as the difference between what one can do independently and what one can do with the assistance of a more able peer or adult. After learning reaches the ZPD level, there is a gradual release of teachers' responsibility as the students are gradually scaffolded while practicing strategies and skills that they eventually accomplish or attain on their own.

A critically important aspect of this literacy program was that students who started the academic year knowing that they were not able to read well *were* able to improve. Alvermann (2001) explains that "if academic literacy instruction is to be effective, it must address issues of self-efficacy and engagement" (p. 6). The students described in this class were highly engaged because they were closely supported and made to realize, with the encouragement of peers and teachers, that they could work through challenging tasks. With this realization, they were motivated to take on other difficult tasks (Bandura, 1997).

Many readers in middle school who struggle with reading remain relatively disengaged from reading tasks. In addition, these students typically have a very low motivation for reading. When teachers give students greater ownership over their own reading experiences—from choosing the books they read to guiding and evaluating their own contributions to the subsequent discussions—students come to value reading as a vital part of their adolescent identity (Raphael, Goatley, McMahon, & Woodman, 1995: Raphael, Kehus, & Damphousse, 2001). That transformation was especially true for the students in the three-period block literacy class.

Building a "community of learners" in a classroom takes a long time, and Mrs. Long and Mrs. Best were highly instrumental in creating and maintaining their community (Allington, 2001). The shared experience of a teacher and a student in a community includes the realization of where "the roles of learner and teacher are shared and the expertise and experience of all participants are respected" (Askew & Lodge, 2001, p. 13). In a close-knit community of learners, such as the one in Mrs. Long and Mrs. Best's classroom, students feel accepted and have a sense of belonging to the whole community. However, as Allington (2001) notes, it's the teachers who are important in creating and maintaining the atmosphere (and thus the community) that supports the literacy environment.

IMPLEMENTING KEY IDEAS

Struggling readers need time to develop as readers in a strong supportive community of learners. The specific characteristics of the three-period block literacy class that helped to improve the reading skills and habits of struggling readers and ultimately created lovers of books included teachers who:

- Foster collaborative and supportive relationships.
- Value discussions in cooperative groups.
- Help students make connections to their real-life experiences.
- Utilize exemplary questioning strategies.
- Teach students to use reading strategies independently.
- Include the wider community of interested others as reading buddies in the classroom.

CONCLUDING THOUGHTS

Middle school is a time of transition for the adolescent. Students have graduated from an elementary school where their one grade-level teacher can adapt to their diverse reading needs and are entering into a new middle school experience where they are expected to learn and grow as readers as they move from teacher to teacher throughout the day. What is needed most for the struggling reading student entering middle school is a community of book lovers created by teachers who can infuse reading instructional time with a sense of enjoyment through an improved curriculum. The three-block literacy class at Glen Bend Middle School provides for this alternative, enabling this fortunate learning community to become confident and independent readers.

CHAPTER SIX

Literacy Leadership in High School
Institutionalizing Literacy in High School Content Areas

Many middle and high school teachers think of themselves as content experts. When I started teaching, I thought of myself as a historian. I wanted to teach history, and I really didn't think much about how students learn. I always focused on content. A lot of secondary teachers enter the field because of their passion for what they are teaching. It's an unusual teacher who comes into secondary education wanting to teach students how to learn. Yet, if we're going to be good teachers, that's really essential.
—Donna Ogle

- -

Jessie, a high school student, walks into her algebra course and sits in the back corner next to her friend Maria. The two of them talk quietly as they pull out their math books. Class begins, and the teacher walks up and down the rows of desks with a clipboard, checking off the names of students who completed their homework. He comes to Jessie and asks if she would flip the homework page over.

"Why didn't you try to finish?" he asks.

"I don't get it," Jessie whispers.

"Well, did you reread the math book? Listen everyone; it's all in the math book! You just need to read the math book! It explains everything and even gives examples."

Jessie looks down at her desk. Concerned, the teacher moves onto Maria.

"Where is your homework?"

"I didn't get it either," Maria explained, "It doesn't make sense."

As class continues, the teacher draws the students' attention to the math book. He reviews the homework and asks the students to turn to the next page of the text. The students are asked to quietly read the paragraphs at the top. Moments later, he meticulously goes through examples of the new math calculations on the whiteboard, refers to the math text, and asks if there are any questions. When no hands are raised, the students are told they can begin their assigned homework.

Maria stops her teacher as he walks up and down the rows to offer assistance.

"Can you help me? I don't understand."

Patiently the teacher explains again and models the calculation on Maria's paper as Jessie looks on. Before leaving to assist a student in the next row, he reminds Maria and Jessie that everything they need to know is written in the book—they just need to reread it. And he was right! Everything *was* written in the book.

The problem was that Maria and Jessie, both second-language learners but grade-level readers, were struggling to understand the academic language in the math book. Without understanding more abstract and complex mathematical terms like *extrapolate*, *factor*, and *irrational number*, problem solving can be difficult. These terms aren't used often outside of math, and if they are not explicitly taught and reviewed, students, including those whose first language is English, can struggle to understand (Goldenberg, 2008; Tompkins, 2010).

A similar scenario could play out in health, science, or history class, but the reality is that reading strategies taught in the content area improve the understanding and achievement of all students, even those who don't usually struggle with reading (Daniels & Zemelman, 2004; Lyons, 2003; Taylor, 2007). As Lyons (2003) points out, "It is the quality of experience and instruction, not the child's brain, that determines success or failure" (pp. 72–73). Without a stockpile of useful reading strategies applied to content areas, some students will inevitably have to struggle to assimilate the content (National Council of Teachers of English [NCTE], 2004). "Literacy in schools has become an equity issue. Children who are unable to get meaning from the printed page will fall further behind in school and in life. Teaching students how to use literacy tools levels the playing field" (G. Niermann, personal communication, August 11, 2010).

In this chapter, we chronicle a reform to institutionalize literacy instruction within content areas in a high school and its school district. Cohorts of teachers participated in a special academic year of learning that included strategic literacy instruction, adolescent development, inquiry, and reflection that was infused into their content teaching and instruction. This chapter recounts the beginning and evolution of the reform program—which resulted in a community of literacy leaders—along with research that explains why it was successful.

Take a look at the same math classroom we just described the following year. Different students fill the seats, now arranged in tables of six, and similar content is taught. As in the previous scenario, the teacher begins the class by checking homework and finds that all students completed the assignment. During this homework review, the teacher asks the students to choose one problem that they found to be the most challenging and then to explain the process they used to determine their answer to the person sitting across from them.

The students know this drill. One of the partners talks while the other listens and comments, and then they switch roles. The teacher pulls his chair from pair to pair as he listens, interjecting his own comments only when needed or when there is a moment to highlight. As the conversations wind down, homework pages are collected by a student and left in the teacher's homework file.

"All right," he announces, "let's continue the homework review with algebra vocabulary theater. I've selected terms and phrases that you should know fairly well, in addition to terms and phrases that you are learning now. When you pick your term out of the hat, use the various resources available to make sure you are on the right track. When I say so, point to one resource in the classroom that you can use. *Point!*"

At once, fingers point to a poster filled with algebraic terms and illustrated definitions, a shelf full of various algebra textbooks, the classroom library that includes tradebooks on math topics, the teacher, and a computer, to name a few possibilities. A generalized buzz ensues as the students choose their vocabulary slips and begin planning. Resources are quickly snatched up as pipe cleaners, small whiteboards, and wooden alphabet blocks rapidly disappear from the classroom prop box.

Later a timer goes off, and the students settle down, continuing to whisper directions to one another. "We only have 20 minutes for your skits—so, let's get started," the teacher interjects. The first pair of girls, Stephie and Carol, ask two classmates to hold up a boa (long fluffy scarf) between them horizontally. A zero hangs from a paper clip in the middle. The room is quiet as Stephie and Carol move equidistant from the zero, both holding a foam numeral five, but the foam five to the left of the zero has a small pencil in front of it to represent a negative number.

Hands shoot into the air, and one of the girls shyly calls on Giovanna, who answers, "Additive inverse, because they make zero. Any number that makes zero—I mean, two numbers that make zero. No, wait." She leans toward her partner, and they whisper briefly. "The additive inverse of five is negative five, because they make zero," she concludes with finality.

"Is she correct?" the teacher asks the class. The class shouts agreement, and the girls sit down as another pair moves up to present the next vocabulary term.

This teacher has transformed his instruction. He has readjusted his teaching methods over the course of a year of intensive study that turned his students into active learners. Two key circumstances account for this teacher's remarkable turnaround, namely, his active participation in his school district's institutionalized literacy reform and, as a direct consequence, his algebra students' much-improved learning attitudes and grades.

The lesson described in the second scenario depicts an instructional experience infused with literacy, with the students no longer viewing academic language as a barrier to their success. The students are provided classroom resources that help them understand algebraic terms, they use the technical vocabulary in their conversations and show that they understand and can apply it as needed, and they know and practice diverse ways of learning algebra (Alverman, Phelps, & Gillis, 2010; Blachowicz & Fisher, 2001; Freeman & Freeman, 2009). Moreover, these students consider themselves a community of learners who actively support one another. They realize that all their peers are learning these new words and concepts alongside them and that some words are easier to learn than others. They speculate about and assess matters with the understanding that they should not rely on their teacher as the sole expert, but rather can trust themselves and one another to learn (Tatum, 2000).

The teacher described in the scenarios improved his pedagogy because of his participation in the Schools' Partnership for Institutional Reform through Adolescent Literacy (SPIRAL). SPIRAL was a "focused, coherent and literacy-based professional development program including reading theory and practice, adolescent development and learning, classroom inquiry and reflection" (LePell, 2003, p. 1) that supported teachers districtwide in making "curricular and instructional choices to improve student literacy in particular and academic performance in general" (p. 1). Those involved in SPIRAL became literacy leaders in their curricular area within the school district.

This chapter describes SPIRAL and the educators who developed it in their quest to significantly improve the academic growth of adolescent students by promoting literacy in the content areas. They focused their efforts in five areas: (1) professional development, (2) student teacher preparation, (3) new teacher support, (4) family and community involvement, (5) improved student learning as a direct consequence of exceptional teaching, and (6) sustaining SPIRAL long-term. First let us describe the community in which the subject high school was located.

THE CASTRO VALLEY COMMUNITY

Castro Valley is a suburb located about 20 minutes from Oakland, California, that features rolling hills, a lagoon, parks, and a strong local economy. The breakdown of the population by ethnicity is 70% Caucasian, 13% Asian, 12% Latino or Hispanic, 5% African American, and 4% other (U.S. Census, 2000). Once best known for its chicken farms, Castro Valley has evolved into a bedroom community that is also the second largest unincorporated area in California ("My Castro Valley History," 2009).

The Castro Valley Unified School District (CVUSD) includes nine elementary schools that feed into two middle schools and one comprehensive high school. In addition, there is an alternative high school and an adult school. Castro Valley High School (CVHS), the main high school and primary setting, is located in a residential neighborhood a few blocks from a major thoroughfare lined with a variety of businesses. Approximately 2,900 students, 130 teachers, and some 45 staff members make up the high school learning community. The academic year is split into two semesters with six periods spanning each school day. On average, less than half of the graduating seniors attend a 4-year college or university, while a bit more than one-third attend a 2-year or vocational school.

FROM HUMBLE BEGINNINGS TO A FIRST-CLASS
LITERACY PROGRAM

Students at CVHS, as at any high school, are expected to read and incorporate useful information in diverse content areas to achieve success. The teachers at CVHS do their best to support students, but the school determined several years ago that more could be done, especially in the area of academic literacy. Fisher and Frey (2004) suggest that, just as student achievement is the responsibility of all content area teachers, then reading should also be the responsibility of all content-area teachers. Providing reading support for both able and struggling students is a vital function for any middle or high school teacher since most find that not all students understand what they read (if they are reading at all)!

At CVHS, the instructional staff was also concerned about students who exhibited "poor reading skills," finding that many of adolescent readers were reluctant and frequently not able to address a wide range of academic reading tasks. At the same time, the teachers lacked the requisite skills and self-confidence to provide their own reading instruction in the specific content areas. Denise Fleming, a faculty member of neighboring Saint Mary's College (SMC) of California's School of Education in the Single Subject Teaching Program, was invited to a CVHS faculty meeting to provide counsel and assistance. Knowing that long-term professional development was the key to implementing positive change, Fleming advocated forming a partnership between the CVUSD and the SMC School of Education, and this partnership became SPIRAL, the Schools' Partnership for Institutional Reform through Adolescent Literacy.

Co-Directors Denise Fleming and Clare LePell, CVHS English department chair, were named along with members of a Steering Committee and Professional Development Committee (PDC) to begin formalizing the partnership. The goal was to create an institutional climate within the school district that supported optimal teaching and learning. LePell recalled, "We were so excited to embark on a collaborative effort to extend and deepen academic literacy" (personal communication, July 25, 2010).

This time frame was when many things began to happen at once. The PDC began to design and later refine a research-based literacy curriculum appropriate for content-area instruction for what the committee members called the "better practices" coursework. At the same time, an application was written with help from the Bay Area School Reform Collaborative (now called Springboard Schools) for funding from the William and Flora Hewlett Foundation. Startup funds were awarded for the first year. The next year three "teaser" Better Practices workshops were offered for interested secondary teachers, and even before the third was presented full funding had been granted for the 3-year SPIRAL project.

In the meantime, faculty members in SMC's Single-Subject Teacher Credential Program wanted to enhance the student teachers' field experiences so that it would be easier for them to apply reading theory and instruction in the classrooms where they were student teaching. Because of the district–college partnership, student teachers from SMC's program were recruited to participate in SPIRAL for their student teaching experience. When selected, they were matched with a supervising teacher from the CVUSD who was also participating in SPIRAL. This partnership supported both practicing and student teachers in creating a supportive literacy framework for content area courses.

After intense committee work, the first cohort began the formal Better Practices coursework the following fall. Each year the steering committee and PDC would meet regularly, both separately and together. In these meetings, committee members came to realize that it was necessary to integrate the unique needs of adolescents into the literacy curriculum, especially given that adolescents are—almost by definition—always "beginning to adopt patterns of thought and behavior that will accompany them for years to come" (Stepp, 2000, p. 3). LePell, perceived correctly from the start that, to achieve success, the SPIRAL curriculum "would have to reflect an understanding of the complex intersecting worlds of adolescence, literacy, teaching, and learning" (LePell, 2002, p. 1). Thus began many years of exemplary professional development devoted to building a cadre of literacy leaders who were able to implement literacy strategies across the broad spectrum of content areas in the district's middle and high schools. Over the years, SPIRAL continued to achieve excellence owing to consistent evaluation, reflection, and its gradual integration into the district's language arts structure.

The PDC was the heart of SPIRAL. The members of the PDC were the co-directors, the Castro Valley school site leaders (the principal and reading specialist or site literacy leader) from each of the district's middle and high schools, and SMC instructors. The SPIRAL steering committee included school site leaders, four leaders from SMC, two secondary student members, two SMC student teachers, two parents of secondary students, two Saint Mary's student teacher supervisors, the district assistant superintendent, and a district administrator.

The structure of SPIRAL was specifically devised and developed to ensure that the most relevant information could be readily shared among students, student teachers, new and veteran teachers, parents, and the community. Parents and students were deliberately included to assist in the work and to help shoulder responsibility for the goal of raising student achievement. This strong infrastructure proved to be the backbone for the continuing quality and success of the program.

Next, let us consider the reform's integration into the schools. Reflecting the complex interconnections of its constituent parts, our analysis of SPIRAL is divided into six sections treating, respectively: (1) professional development; (2) student teacher preparation; (3) support for teachers new to the district's middle and high schools; (4) the involvement of whole families and the whole community; (5) improvements in student learning attributable to SPIRAL strategies; and (6) sustaining SPIRAL long-term. To conclude the chapter we present some of the reasons for SPIRAL's success.

PROFESSIONAL DEVELOPMENT

This section describes the SPIRAL model and the subsequent professional development experience that was created to meet the unique needs of the district. The model included the two main SPIRAL committees—the Steering Committee and the Professional Development Committee—consisting of representatives from each school. The Better Practices seminars and the teacher cohorts are explained here as well.

The Steering Committee

The 25-member SPIRAL Steering Committee was composed of the project directors, district personnel, site leaders from each Castro Valley middle and high school, SMC School of Education representatives, and parent representatives. The purpose of this committee was to consistently communicate with the college, the district, individual schools, and the community to ensure that all information relating to SPIRAL was properly and widely disseminated. The committee's tasks included discussing and approving the annual budget, filing grant reports, and adequately evaluating the program. In later years, the committee took on the additional task of creating workshops beyond the scope of the Better Practices seminars for anyone interested in such topics as media awareness or informational literacy.

Meeting first monthly and then quarterly, the Steering Committee helped SPIRAL to reflect on its past and look to its future. It helped sustain the enthusiasm of, and ensured adequate participation by, all stakeholders and maintained the organization's most effective attributes and strengths while cultivating new and expanding functions in order to reach more students.

One of these new functions was to provide the community with a series of parent education events that focused on key adolescent issues like depression and drug use. The parent members of the Steering Committee created and organized these events with the help of SPIRAL PDC members and SPIRAL cohort alumni. The topics treated in these sessions reflected adolescents' need and interests, and expert commentators were occasionally invited to participate.

The Professional Development Committee

Composed of 10 literacy leaders from Saint Mary's School of Education and the Castro Valley secondary schools, the PDC was the organizing force behind the SPIRAL courses and workshops for teachers, students, and parents. Committee members changed over the years, but a dedicated core group of teacher leaders remained on the committee, helping to connect the past, present, and future of SPIRAL's work.

The main purpose of the PDC was to design, implement, follow up, coordinate, and evaluate the SPIRAL programs and workshops over the course of each academic year and over time. The committee also developed a professional library, coached and collaborated with SPIRAL participants, recruited future participants, and kept detailed records of their work.

As part of SPIRAL's mission, the PDC set forth a theoretical framework and epistemology that served as a foundation for everything SPIRAL sought to accomplish. In general, such concepts as schema theory (Anderson, 2004), constructivism (Fosnot, 1996), metacognition (Paris, Wasik, & Turner, 1991), the zone of proximal development (Vygotsky, 1978), and scaffolding (Bruner, 1986) guided the committee's deliberations and decisions. Based on this underlying foundation, a list of topics was issued to guide the coursework each year, including such matters as literacy strategies, study skills, class climate, and adolescent development.

In addition to the professional development, "reading school" skills were developed. LePell (2004) noted early on that "in order to 'read school' effectively, adolescents need to be taught—and they need to practice—the elements of good studentship" (p. 1). The study skills needed to "read school" effectively were included in the SPIRAL coursework, incorporating such good practices and habits as managing one's time wisely, knowing whom to ask for help, and carefully assessing each teacher's class expectations individually.

Another task undertaken by the PDC was to develop the format, guidelines, supervisory details, and evaluation of the focal student assignment. Described in much greater detail later, this assignment gave cohort teachers the opportunity to focus on what they were learning with a particular student who would benefit from individualized one-on-one sessions designed to meet the student's unique needs. These one-on-one sessions proved to be highly successful in accelerating learning.

Evaluation was considered an important committee responsibility, and therefore evaluation data were collected often and taken seriously by the committee. PDC members fully appreciated that analyzing and following up on the evaluation data from the various SPIRAL projects would help propel SPIRAL's growth as well as promote genuine change. For example, the PDC sponsored a CVHS teacher training session aimed at helping students "read school" better by learning a few key literacy strategies. The training session, already well received, became a highly attended function each time it was offered.

Site Coordinators

Saint Mary's School of Education and the district's various middle and high schools each had a SPIRAL liaison person or site coordinator whose main function was to report any school site SPIRAL activities, give his or her own input, report back to the site faculty, and promote SPIRAL and its various projects. The coordinators and liaisons were kept very busy. Their accomplishments are chronicled in sample reports provided in Tables 6.1 and 6.2.

Better Practice Seminars

Each year the PDC designed 11–13 formal 2-hour instructional sessions known as Better Practices seminars (see Figure 6.1). The session's content was based on literacy theory and research, the needs of cohorts, evaluations of cohorts from previous years, and the recommendations of experts. During summer meetings, the committee would develop a plan detailing the scope and sequence of projected topics as well as a draft of the course content for each of the following year's sessions.

The content of each session was carefully planned and organized into six categories: (1) the goal for the session; (2) the topic of the lesson; (3) the strategy du jour;

TABLE 6.1. Castro Valley High School Site Coordinator Report: January through March

Site activities

1. Continued informal coaching assistance to Cohorts [i.e., Groups] 1–3.
2. Continued informal discussions about adolescent development and particular teaching strategies with members of all cohorts years 1–3, as well as staff members considering the Better Practices course as a future activity.
3. Planned lessons with members of Cohort 3.
4. Designed and facilitated a session on equity issues.
5. Involved in constructing and maintaining a coherent classroom environment.
6. Designed and taught demonstration lessons.
7. Observed cohort members.

Site communication

1. Published newsletter for all cohort members.
2. Distributed and posted reminders for upcoming Better Practices sessions and focal student data collection.

Representation

1. Participated in School Site Literacy team meetings as the SPIRAL representative.
2. Reported about SPIRAL's ongoing activities to the CVHS Advisory Committee each month.
3. Attended SPIRAL Professional Development Committee meetings.

Student teachers

1. Welcomed student teachers who are starting training in the spring term.
2. Opened classrooms to student teacher observations.
3. Helped student teachers navigate the district and CVHS systems of management.

TABLE 6.2. Saint Mary's College School of Education Liaison Report: January through March

SPIRAL evaluation

"Rethinking SPIRAL" meeting hosted by Saint Mary's College. Those in attendance included the Dean of the School of Education, Single-Subject Program Director, Saint Mary's SPIRAL liaisons, and representatives from the SPIRAL Professional Development Committee, Steering Committee, Castro Valley Unified School District, and Castro Valley schools' parent committees.

Student teachers

Support for student teachers involved (1) a refresher on reading strategies, (2) the use of student log books to document observations and implementation of reading strategies, and (3) the creation of a self-evaluation file that included samples and feedback.

New state law

A new California law affects the organization of teacher training programs. Our school partnership setup is in compliance with the new law.

Welcome
to Training Cohort 3 of . . .
SPIRAL

Schools' **P**artnership for **I**nstitutional **R**eform through **A**dolescent **L**iteracy

Dates for the School Year:

CVHS Library, 4:00–6:00 P.M., Thursday Meetings

Sept. 20, Oct. 4, Oct. 18, Nov. 1, Nov. 15, Dec. 6, Jan 17, Feb. 14, Feb. 28, Mar. 14, Mar. 28, April 11, May 9

This course is brought to you by the Professional Development Committee of SPIRAL, Schools' Partnership for Institutional Reform through Adolescent Literacy, a partnership between CVUSD and Saint Mary's College School of Education funded by a grant from the Hewlett Foundation.

FIGURE 6.1. Meeting dates for SPIRAL Cohort 3.

(4) a discussion of work with focal students; (5) personal reflections; and (6) suggested preparations for the next session (see Figure 6.2). Sessions were facilitated by SPIRAL's PDC and former cohort members. Each "class" was interactive, combining small-group, whole-class, and individual work as well as reflections along with sufficient time to build a sense of community through the sharing of accolades, conversation, and meals or snacks. Figure 6.3 presents a sample detailed agenda from a March Better Practices class.

The Cohorts

Each spring and summer, teachers were recruited in all content areas for the Better Practices program from the district's middle and high school sites. Because the district supported SPIRAL so strongly, the teachers involved were able to apply their cohort coursework toward their salary schedule, just like taking a graduate course. Those who were interested formed an informal teacher cohort that studied together during the whole academic year. Participants experienced, implemented, and reflected upon research-based literacy instruction designed specifically to gain knowledge and guidance in dealing with adolescent development and related teen issues (Hyde, 1992).

Throughout the sessions, the teacher cohorts worked and learned in small and large groups. They began using a common vocabulary that could be used to discuss reading and writing across all content areas and with other teachers irrespective of their expertise. They also had the opportunity to self-evaluate their professional and personal growth as a result of their participation in SPIRAL. Gemma Niermann, an adjunct professor from SMC reflects:

> "I was talking to a cohort member who was reflecting on her learning and teaching experiences. One example was that she learned it was most important to establish some kind of connection with every student. She had 70 students in

Better Practices Session 2

A. Goal	Participants perceive how their student learners are influenced by adolescence.
B. Topic	Adolescent Developmental Needs and Necessary Adaptations (This program will include a briefing on the selected readings and students' pictorials.)
C. Strategy du Jour	ReQuest (Manzo, 1969).
D. Focal Students	Revisit the issues of diversity and varying skill levels.
	Share potential focal student selections.
E. Personal Reflection	Reflect on student pictorials, assigned readings, and reading strategies.
F. Next Time	Read about the literacy process. Think about the challenges of vocabulary acquisition in your subject area, the varying success of individual students, and speculate about what accounts for the variations. Bring a textbook containing challenging vocabulary. Select your focal student.

Session 3

A. Goal	Participants understand the role of vocabulary in text comprehension.
B. Topic	Vocabulary in the Content Area
C. Strategies du Jour	Vocabulary illustrations/bookmarks
	Semantic mapping
D. Focal Students	Why did you select him or her? What baseline data are available to track progress? How can we collect additional data?
E. Personal Reflection	Reflect on focal student selection, assigned readings, and vocabulary strategies.
F. Next Time	Read articles on comprehension. Obtain permission from parents for focal student research. Choose a pseudonym for your selected focal student.

FIGURE 6.2. Professional Development Committee course content draft for SPIRAL Sessions 2 and 3.

her chorus classes and understood that the choral concept of one voice, along with matching outfits when performing, took away students' uniqueness. This teacher used journal writing to get to know each student as an individual, and in responding to their journal entries, made those connections with students and felt she made each feel important. She found it was a great way to find out who they were and what they were thinking" (personal communication, July 25, 2010).

Finally, graduates continued to stay involved in SPIRAL. Many helped to facilitate Better Practices sessions for subsequent cohorts, some became members of the SPIRAL committees, and others became school site leaders. Their classroom doors were open to those who wanted to observe key literacy strategies in action, and many welcomed student teachers not only from SMC but also from other colleges and universities as well. The inspiring work of the cohort members helped the SPIRAL project attain its goal of establishing a communitywide institutional climate that supported optimal teaching and learning methods.

Class 10
Thursday, March 22

Goal: Participants will understand the need for and the relationship between protocols and individual literacy strategies.

Announcements

Roll sheets

Refreshments

Kudos

A. TOPIC: LITERACY STRATEGIES AND A PROTOCOL

1. Introduction to the lesson:
   a. The difference between a strategy and a protocol.
      Strategy: a conscious plan
      Protocol: a treatment that harnesses the power of a strategy
   b. Working with strategies (like mapping, KWL, cloze) anchored in our understanding of protocols.
   c. Working with protocols
      What are our principles? What is our overarching goal?
      How can we construct a developmentally and culturally appropriate treatment plan with the depth and breadth that can last for the long haul?
2. EXAMPLE of a Protocol: **THINK-ALOUD**
   a. Background: based upon metacognition
   b. The ability to *think about one's thinking*
   c. Teacher models thinking out loud as one would approach the text
   d. Modeling for your students, using an eighth-grade text:
      I'm going to read this out loud to you.
      I'm going to be engaging in metacognition.
      I'm going to show you what competent readers do.
      I'm going to show you what happens inside my head.
      You need to listen.
      Watch how I'm drawing this out on the board—maps, lines, words, questions, definitions, predictions, etc.
      I will talk about what is going on in my head.
   e. PRACTICE in your group: 1. Underline vocabulary. 2. Decide what you will say.
   f. Question: What did your group wonder about?
   g. Think: **In my content area,** how can I use thinking aloud in an appropriate way to see how my mind processes the material in the text that I'm asking THEM to process?
   h. Plan for instruction
      Individually use the text you brought to plan and extend instruction.
         How will you process FOR *your* students?
         How much will you have *them* process the text?
         How will they process . . . in pairs, threes?
         How much advance preparation is necessary?
         When will you bring them back together?
         What words will you choose?
         What kinds of words would you post around the room?
   i. Closure: Reflect on think-alouds and what you learned

(cont.)

FIGURE 6.3. Agenda for SPIRAL Better Practices Class 10, given in March.

B. Personal Reflection
   a. Concretize the experience you just had.
   b. Answer in your journal: *How do you envision using a think-aloud in one or more of your classes?* If you can cite the text you just used or plan to use, that would be helpful to the SPIRAL Professional Development Committee.

C. Student Work
   a. Presentation of student work in concept mapping.
   b. Briefing on focal student successes.
   c. Practice the strategies and protocols we're learning.

D. Announcements and Preparations for Next Session
   a. Next Session: April 5th, The Reading–Writing Connection
   b. Additional Session: April 26th, Film as Text
       Visual media also constitute a text that needs to be read and analyzed. It needs to be unpacked and understood. This additional session will provide a special focus on video—how do you access factual information in a visual text, and how does the text lead you to expectations? We'll also look at biases and the images one chooses to show to others.
   c. End of the Year
       Interviews: Your site leader will make an appointment with you.
       Journals: These are part of our accountability materials on classroom practice and the affective aspect of teaching.
       Student work: This material constitutes further documentation of your student's achievement.

FIGURE 6.3. *(cont.)*

STUDENT TEACHER PREPARATION

Single-subject credential candidates from SMC were invited to apply to participate in the SPIRAL program as part of their student teaching experience (see Figure 6.4 for the text of the publicity brochure). They had the opportunity to first observe at Castro Valley's middle and high schools, which included visits to the rooms of teachers who had participated in the Better Practices seminars. If the student teachers were interested, they could fill out an application form (see Figure 6.5). If they were accepted into the program, they would receive a stipend of $1,000 to assist with travel expenses and to compensate them for the additional time that would be required to fulfill their obligations as part of the partnership.

Student teachers accepted to the SPIRAL literacy partnership would be paired with SMC supervisors and strong master teachers who had completed the Better Practices coursework. The student teachers would also be considered an integral part of the SPIRAL program and would be expected to attend the meetings and take a leadership role in working with struggling readers and writers.

As part of their credential coursework at SMC, single-subject candidates customarily took a reading course irrespective of their content-area specialty. If the candidate was accepted to become part of the SPIRAL partnership, not only would the student teach, but also he or she could take their SMC reading course during the day at CVHS and have it explicitly connected to the teaching they were observing and undertaking.

Schools' **P**artnership for **I**nstitutional **R**eform through **A**dolescent **L**iteracy = **SPIRAL**
A literacy-based partnership between Saint Mary's College and Castro Valley Unified School District

SINGLE-SUBJECT STUDENTS

- Are you interested in participating in an experimental student teaching placement aimed at improving adolescent literacy?
- Are you looking for ways to better integrate your coursework and field placements to maximize your effectiveness?
- Have you wondered how you could make a difference in the school reform movement?
- Are you interested in earning $1,000?

Saint Mary's College and Castro Valley Unified School District have created SPIRAL, a project aimed at improving adolescent literacy across the curriculum in grades 6–12. Castro Valley Unified secondary teachers participate in year-long programs of professional development and meaningful parent activities. We are seeking a limited number of committed student teachers from all content areas to engage in collaborative field placements in Castro Valley secondary schools.

Collaboration: You will have an opportunity to work closely with other student teachers in and out of class.

Support: You will have the support of a master teacher participating in a professional development program. You will also have increased contact with your course instructor and your college supervisor.

Relevance: You will take SCED 253C (Secondary Reading) in Castro Valley during the school day and apply the content in a focused clinical setting in your subject area.

Incentive: You will be guaranteed a job interview with a Castro Valley Unified School District Administrator and a $1,000 stipend for participating in the program.

ALL SUBJECT MATTERS ARE WELCOME!

Requirements:

- Good standing in the Single-Subject Program
- Ability to be in your placement for an entire semester
- Ability to attend SCED 235C in Castro Valley during the school day and apply the content in a focused clinical setting
- Ability to attend weekly collaboration and planning sessions with other student teachers
- Ability to attend conferences and other activities related to SPIRAL and the Bay Area School Reform Collaborative

FIGURE 6.4. Brochure to publicize the SPIRAL partnership to SMC student teachers.

As part of their SMC reading course, the student teacher credential candidates participated in an intensive 15-hour tutorial with a struggling reader who was serving as a focal student. Candidates assessed their focal students and then analyzed the assessments to develop a unique literacy program for each student. This program of intervention strategies, taught in the SMC reading course, enabled the focal students to accelerate their learning and the SMC student teachers to better connect theory with practice, thereby integrating their coursework with their teaching.

As a result of their hard work and commitment, all SMC student teachers were guaranteed an interview for any openings in the district. Often, when SMC student teachers

Date: _____

Name: _____

Telephone: _____

E-mail: _____

Content Area: _____

Location of Any Other Student Teaching Placement: _____

Semester for Which You Are Applying: _____

Please attach to this application a brief essay of approximately 300 words addressing the following question: If you were to be part of a positive movement for change in the schools, what form would it take?

Forward applications to Dr. Gemma Niermann at the School of Education.

FIGURE 6.5. SPIRAL application form for student teachers.

were hired for a CVUSD position, they continued to be involved in SPIRAL through Better Practices coursework or helping with committee work. They were also paired with new SMC student teachers for a term. This partnership enabled the two to share similar experiences, but more importantly to closely explore the relationship between theory, coursework, and practice.

SUPPORT FOR TEACHERS NEW TO THE DISTRICT'S MIDDLE AND HIGH SCHOOLS

Each year new teachers were welcomed into the CVUSD community. Many of these new teachers had just completed their credential coursework and consequently were required to participate in the California State Beginning Teacher Support and Assessment (BTSA) program. At the time, BTSA was a 2-year induction program funded by the state of California and supported by both the California Department of Education and the California Commission on Teacher Credentialing (CCTC). It created the opportunity for fledgling K–12 teachers to improve their teaching practices while transitioning to the many responsibilities of being a fully independent teacher. Upon their completion of the program, the teachers earned a Clear Teaching Credential (California Commission on Teacher Credentialing, 2006).

Clare LePell gave presentations in the BTSA program that communicated the benefits of participating in SPIRAL programs to the newest teachers in the district. Beginning teachers, after earning a Clear Teaching Credential, were encouraged to enroll in the year-long cohort study, and a few did. Michelle was a new teacher who enrolled in SPIRAL. She explained:

"SPIRAL is a lifesaver. I went to the SPIRAL classes, and what I learned I use all the time: three levels of reading, close reading, KWLs. I use the strategies every week! All my lessons are centered on some SPIRAL-based technique. Now that I've been teaching a while, ... I wish I could take those classes all over again. I think SPIRAL should be a part of all beginning teacher programs. And for the students, they learn [these strategies] their freshman year, and then they don't stop using [the strategies] until they leave.... They do them more and more, and I think it forces them to get better, you know?"

Michelle felt strongly about the positive effects of SPIRAL. She explained that her first 3 years of teaching were tough, and she considered leaving the profession. With the support she received, especially from SPIRAL, she was able to "put it all together" and realize "what's happening" in the educational life of an adolescent, which, in turn, made her a better educator.

Focal Student Experience

In addition to implementing SPIRAL work with whole classes of students, both SPIRAL teachers and student teachers chose one student with whom they could create an intensive learning partnership that would allow them to assess the effectiveness of their instruction while also improving the student's performance and achievement levels. Teachers worked with their focal student one-on-one to implement the academic, affective, and literacy aspects of SPIRAL.

As SPIRAL began each fall, participants chose a student who would benefit from a one-on-one intervention that—collectively—would reflect the diversity of the school district. When a student was selected, the parents were asked not only to give their permission for his or her participation (see Figures 6.6 and 6.7) but also to join the teacher in actively supporting the student's development.

As teachers worked with their focal students, they taught, assessed, and analyzed, collecting data to allow for meaningful instruction, interpersonal connections, and positive interactions. By using their Better Practices knowledge about literacy and adolescent development, the impact of this one-on-one work was usually far-reaching and long-lasting.

One Success Story

Peter was the focal student in a high school English class whose teacher was in SPIRAL. He was failing most of his classes and was getting a D– in English. With the help of SPIRAL, Peter's English teacher developed a plan with Peter and his parents to communicate weekly. The improved communications allowed Peter's parents to support his learning better at home. They appreciated the additional communications, began to feel more comfortable with the school, and attended several SPIRAL sessions intended for parents whenever they were able to do so.

September 29

Dear Mr. and Mrs. Jones,

I am Sandra Knoss and your son, Mikel, is in my history class. You may have read in the newspapers or heard through the PTSA that Castro Valley's middle and high schools have created a partnership project with Saint Mary's College called SPIRAL (Schools' Partnership for Institutional Reform through Adolescent Literacy). The goal of the partnership is to help all students in grades 6–12 become better readers, writers, and thinkers in all subject areas.

Through SPIRAL, I am participating in a year-long course aimed at improving adolescent literacy. In addition to looking at new and different ways to improve whole-class instruction, teachers are focusing on how to help meet the needs of individual students.

I am writing to ask your permission to work with Mikel as my focal student for the course. By working one-on-one with your child, I hope to see how the study of adolescence and literacy instruction can improve the achievement of my students and my teaching.

Your student's participation in this project may involve some or all the the following activities:

- We will meet together one-on-one to discuss (1) his progress in my class, (2) the literacy strategies I am using with him, and (3) the project in general.
- I will collect and share work samples from class with Mikel.
- I will share, through discussion and writing, Mikel's progress with my colleagues in the SPIRAL project.
- I will never use Mikel's name but instead use a pseudonym to ensure complete confidentiality.
- I may also share Mikel's work and accomplishments with others via talks, presentations at conferences, or manuscripts for publication—always, however, keeping his real identity a secret.

If you would like to discuss this matter further before making a decision, please feel free to contact me immediately. At any time during your child's participation in the project I will also be happy to discuss any questions or concerns you or Mikel may have about the project.

Please keep this information page and return the attached permission form [reproduced as Figure 6.7] to me.

Thank you.

FIGURE 6.6. Sample letter to the parent or guardian of a focal student, requesting permission for the student's participation.

During their one-on-one sessions, Peter and his teacher talked about everything from his classes to situations with girls. Over time, Peter became more confident, participated in class regularly, and improved all of his course grades, receiving mostly C's. His parents were happy about the consistent communications that better enabled them to support Peter at home, and they were impressed with his increased motivation and much-improved grades at school.

Although each case is unique, Peter's English teacher found that positive feedback was essential to spurring Peter's motivation and academic improvement, while open and honest communications with both Peter and his parents helped too. Peter was given additional materials for all his courses to keep at home, allowing him to prepare in advance of the lessons in his classes and to review them better afterward. He knew he had adults both at home and at school who were keeping tabs on him to help celebrate his accomplishments and support both his academic and emotional needs.

Dear Mrs. Franklin,

I, <u>Margie Jones</u>, give my permission for my son, Mikel Jones, to participate in the SPIRAL project. I understand that he/she will be a focal student in your class. I also understand that my son/daughter's participation in this project may involve some or all of the following activities:

Meeting with you to discuss his/her progress in your class, the literacy strategies you are using, and the project in general
Collecting and keeping work samples
Sharing, through discussion and writing, my son's/daughter's progress with your colleagues in the SPIRAL project
Using a pseudonym to ensure confidentiality at all times

You may share my son's/daughter's work and accomplishments with others via talks, presentations at conferences, or manuscripts for publication, always keeping his/her real identity a secret.

I understand I can contact you at any time to discuss my child's participation in the project. I further understand that I may withdraw my permission for my son/daughter to participate at any time by sending a letter to you indicating my desire.

_____
Parent's signature and date

_____
Student's signature and date

FIGURE 6.7. Sample of a focal student parent permission form.

FAMILY AND COMMUNITY INVOLVEMENT

SPIRAL cohorts credit both the community and students' families as vital components of their success. Parents, community members, and the Parent Teacher and Student Association (PTSA) president actively participated in the SPIRAL Steering Committee. They were empowered to develop and implement a series of parent education evenings focusing on various topics of special interest to adolescents. They even arranged a special presentation treating the academic and social life of the typical adolescent that was specifically intended for the parents of the district's fourth and fifth graders.

Another important aspect of SPIRAL was the involved teachers and parents' greater inclination to engage more frequently with other parents and guardians. Parents who might otherwise have stayed out of their adolescent child's academic world altogether were invited to become a vital part of it. This open communication proved to be a positive stimulus in the lives of many students and their families.

IMPROVED STUDENT LEARNING AS A DIRECT CONSEQUENCE OF EXCEPTIONAL TEACHING

Because of SPIRAL's wide influence, Castro Valley students were made extraordinarily aware of their own literacy. They consciously built on their prior knowledge, used reading strategies in a variety of courses, demonstrated metacognitive awareness, and shared a common literacy vocabulary with their peers and teachers. Anne Parris, a SPIRAL teacher and longtime PDC member, observed that "SPIRAL has had a very positive effect. Students are processing linguistically in ways most of us would not have considered viable a few years ago" (personal communication, June 2, 2010).

In the end, Castro Valley students became better able to learn new concepts as a result of their use of reading strategies. They became much more adept at "reading school" because they were institutionally supported in acquiring new organizational and learning skills. Furthermore, they acquired better communication skills by speaking more with the adults most central to their academic and personal lives. These accomplishments, in turn, boosted their self-confidence and sense of achievement. In fact, the students' parents were so pleased with the success of SPIRAL programs that they campaigned to include all incoming high school freshmen in "reading school" training, which took place before school began in the fall, furthering the goal of institutionalizing SPIRAL.

In surveys, students were very positive about their learning experiences while in the classes of SPIRAL trained teachers. They practiced the reading strategies so often at school and at home that they largely internalized the underlying purposes and procedures. In one class, 75% of the students could clearly articulate a new strategy's purposes and procedures the day after learning it, and more than half agreed that the strategy would be useful in their future coursework.

SPIRAL: NEXT STEPS

The visionaries who created and contributed to SPIRAL extended their efforts even as the funding from the 3-year grant ended. Given the large number of SPIRAL-trained teacher leaders, the district only had to look within for effective professional development for years to come. Continuing the focus on institutional reform, two areas were targeted. First, there was sustained professional development for SPIRAL cohort members, and, second, there were ongoing professional development workshops featuring both cutting-edge and traditional research-based strategies for the teachers of adolescents.

Sustaining SPIRAL cohort members was beneficial so that they could not only maintain their effectiveness in the classroom but also acquire skills based on different, recently developed, or newly innovative strategies. They continued to support one another informally but also participated in organized gatherings ranging from friendly reunions to professional meetings and workshops.

Ongoing professional development workshops (see Figure 6.8 for a sampling of topics) were created by SPIRAL members for all the teachers of adolescents as well as interested parents. These workshops generally highlighted the reading strategies and practices that were judged to be of greatest interested to SPIRAL-trained teachers as well as teachers new to the district. Also developed for SPIRAL Next Steps was a multicultural literature collection. Book titles and interest levels ranged from kindergarten, to young adult, to teacher resources. The list of selections available to teachers included

LITERACY STRATEGY

KWL (Ogle, 1986)

This workshop models active thinking and helps teachers prepare students to read expository and/or difficult text. The letters *K*, *W*, and *L* stand for the three activities in which students typically engage while reading to learn, namely, recalling what they *K*now, determining what they *W*ant to learn, and identifying what they *L*earn as they read. Designed to help teachers create an effective before-, during-, and after-lesson, this workshop should help students to predict, anticipate, organize, and reorganize information as they read. This workshop is applicable to all subject areas and can be a valuable experience for educators and parents alike.

STUDY SKILL

"Reading" Different Classes and Teacher Expectations

In this workshop, participants see how they can help students negotiate the many "playing fields" in a large school. Participants review a "Know Your Classes" handout and discuss how students can be helped to better understand their new courses and teachers' diverse expectations. This workshop is best suited to teachers of incoming sixth or ninth graders and to parents interested in making a stronger connection to secondary school.

CLASS CLIMATE

Creating a Human Rights-Centered Classroom

This workshop provides practical strategies for classroom management that help create a community of respect and mutual responsibility. Activities include taking the human rights "temperature" of a classroom or school setting, planning for the first days of school, and working to support a student-centered learning environment. This workshop is appropriate for educators and support staff at all levels.

ADOLESCENT DEVELOPMENT/ADULT EDUCATION

A Tribe Apart

This workshop examines the underlying lessons in the individual profiles featured in Hersch's (1998–1999) *A Tribe Apart: A Journey into the Heart of the American Adolescent*. Depending on the audience, the workshop could highlight individual chapters in the book or look at the overarching messages embedded in the young people's experiences. The chief focus of the session is to discuss the ways in which real communication between teenagers and adults can be encouraged and enriched and ways in which the Castro Valley community can become more of "a village" determined to raise healthy children through meaningful cooperation among adults.

FIGURE 6.8. Sample of SPIRAL professional development topics. The workshops described above were conducted for various audiences and in diverse formats, such as cohort coursework, staff meetings, voluntary workshops, and evening community presentations.

the book title, author, grade level, International Standard Book Number (ISBN), and short summary.

WHY SPIRAL WORKED

SPIRAL was an exemplary educational project for a wide variety of reasons. From the outset, its organizers had a clear idea of what they sought to accomplish, how it was to be accomplished, and what might ensure its success over time (Ogle, 2007). The goals

of addressing adolescent students' literacy instruction and teachers' professional development in literacy instruction were always uppermost in mind as the initial committee
members began their planning. Because of these goals, higher-quality student outcomes
were ultimately achieved owing to the consistent long-term multicurricular work of the
SPIRAL participants (Joyce & Showers, 2002).

Most all of SPIRAL's participants were serious about their determination to change
the lives of adolescents for the better. The responsibilities connected with SPIRAL were
shared with SMC School of Education instructors, who helped determine which reading
strategies would be best suited to any given course (Schneider, 1992) as well as facilitating instructional sessions and committee work (Hyde, 1992; Hyde & Pink, 1992; Pink &
Hyde, 1992). What was critical, though, was that the professional development provided
for the cohorts was based on the distinctive needs of the teachers and adolescents in the
local school district.

The high quality of the SPIRAL program and its instruction derived directly from
the adults' dedication to adolescent students' unmet reading aspirations. The quality of
the teachers' instruction in the classroom directly reflected the amount of time SPI-
RAL teachers were given to learn, practice, understand, and synthesize their knowledge
(Barth, 2000). Of course, it wasn't all work—many teachers, in fact, reported that it was
a great deal of fun (Lyons, 2003)!

Another reason why SPIRAL was successful was that it focused on institutional
change within schools and across the district instead of aiming at changes in individuals
alone (Pink & Hyde, 1992). This shared knowledge, repertoire, and academic language
allowed teachers to work as teams within and across schools to make the lessons learned
in SPIRAL have future applications in planning the next year's classes and coursework
(Barth, 2000; Gaskins, 2005; Lyons, 2003; Ogle, 2007). Teacher teams were able to
collaboratively analyze and rethink old routines, striving for increasingly better ways to
support students in learning and understanding (Hyde, 1992).

SPIRAL cohort members became literacy leaders in their respective schools, sharing their enhanced understanding with their colleagues and in the ensuing debate further
deepening their own understanding in turn (Joyce & Showers, 2002; Schmidt, Sharp, &
Stephens, 2001). As literacy leaders, they had a vested interest in assisting colleagues in
developing literacy in any content area where adolescents still struggled to understand.
In that context, achieving even partial success was a victory for all. As SPIRAL literacy
leaders spread to numerous school sites, a significant grassroots educational movement
was realized.

Participation in SPIRAL was voluntary across the district, but this aspect was also
a positive benefit in explaining its success. Teachers participated because they *wanted
to be there*, and many continued to play a major role in shaping improved learning during
subsequent years. This enhanced sense of ownership helped to sustain meaningful institutional reform in teaching practices for years thereafter (Fogarty & Pete, 2007).

Parental support was also extremely important. Taylor (2007) and Gaskins (2005)
observe that, when encouraged to be active in their children's academic and emotional

lives, parents form a special bond with the school community, thus reinforcing students' learning, motivation, achievement, and development. Parents are then drawn further into the school community, and their involvement usually continues to increase—as it did with the parents of many focus students. This development turns into a win–win situation for the parents and their children, because both are provided with the assistance that leads to greater achievement and success.

The CVUSD unhesitatingly endorsed SPIRAL, and the success of the program was heralded by local education administrators. Each year when SPIRAL cohorts formally graduated with a Certificate of Completion, even school board members attended the ceremony to honor and commend the graduates. SPIRAL's accomplishments were celebrated by all stakeholders who recognized its success.

IMPLEMENTING KEY IDEAS

Successfully incorporating better reading strategies into diverse academic courses is a worthy goal, but SPIRAL also provided a framework for *institutionalizing* literacy reform. Key ideas for implementation include:

- Beginning with a research-based plan to incorporate change and reform.
- Building partnerships with educators, administrators, researchers, professors, parents, and students to support planning, implementation, and evaluation.
- Forming committees to distribute the workload.
- Researching and applying for grants and other funding.
- Evaluating one's progress objectively and reflecting frequently.
- Encouraging the *long-term* involvement of the participants.

CONCLUDING THOUGHTS

In writing this chapter, we visited many of the educators who were originally involved in founding and running SPIRAL. Their present-day reaction to the program remained much the same as always, namely, "SPIRAL changed my life." SPIRAL transformed the way they taught, regardless of the specific content area under consideration, and this transformation resulted in active participation and engaged learning from the students because of the conscious integration of literacy. SPIRAL left an indelible mark on many teachers and students, one that will benefit them throughout their respective careers.

PART III

LITERACY LEADERSHIP IN SCHOOLWIDE CONTEXTS

CHAPTER SEVEN

Implementing Technology to Support Readers

If we teach today as we taught yesterday, we rob our children of tomorrow.

—JOHN DEWEY

Technology integration is changing education so fast, there is no room for complacency.
—SISTER KATHLEEN DONNELLY, principal, Sacred Heart School

Emily Fogarty is a veteran teacher with 8 years of experience at Sacred Heart School. She is an elementary teacher who embraces the use of technology in her daily classroom life. Technology is not something she does but something that is part of the fabric of her classroom. She has clear expectations and outcomes for her fourth-grade students, and they understand her expectations. Her lessons are engaging, relevant, and personalized, empowering students to take charge of their own learning. Her teaching is focused on what the students need to know and how best to engage them in learning.

Emily's interactive science lessons incorporate the use of the Smart Board, an interactive whiteboard with a touch-sensitive screen that works in conjunction with a computer and a projector, along with individual student computers. The focus of one lesson, "Five-Kingdom" Classification System, included advanced vocabulary and reading expository text. Emily organized this lesson by making thoughtful decisions and integrating technology to engage all the learners.

The faculty at Sacred Heart is committed to integrating technology into every aspect of the curriculum, with the purpose of engaging all learners and supporting all readers. Teachers, with the support of the principal and technology specialist, are able to customize content for students in the classroom. The goal, according to the technology specialist, is to make technology invisible and the content extraordinarily visible.

Our purpose in this chapter is, first, to explore the technology journey at Sacred Heart School and show how one elementary school has successfully integrated technology into the curriculum to support readers. Then we review the research underlying the integration of technology into the curriculum to create engaging and meaningful lessons using authentic contexts. Next, the challenging role of the teacher in this time of rapid change is explored, and class lessons that employ such technology as the SMART board, iPod Touches, individual computers, and Internet search engines are discussed. Finally we present a few key ideas for successfully implementing technology supportive of all readers.

SACRED HEART SCHOOL

Sacred Heart is a small private school located in Winnetka, Illinois, a northern suburb of Chicago. The school houses 300 students from junior kindergarten through eighth grade, boasting an average class size of only 17 students. Sacred Heart's academic programs are designed to stimulate intellectual curiosity, develop critical thinking, and foster the desire for lifelong learning. The school was designated an Apple Distinguished School (*www.sacredheart-winnetka.org/academics/academics.html#reco*) for 2009–2010 in recognition of its success in implementing a 21st-century vision of education. As one of only 54 schools nationwide to be recognized that year, it was the only private Catholic elementary school in the country to receive this honor.

The core curriculum at Sacred Heart is focused on reading, mathematics, physical sciences, social sciences, and religion. This core curriculum is supplemented with courses in Spanish, art, music, physical education, and technology integration. Even though technology is fully integrated into each classroom, some classes take place in the school's computer lab.

The computer lab at Sacred Heart is a state-of-the-art resource. Students in grades K–5 are introduced to appropriate technology by, for example, assembling an interactive report, organizing a podcast, and conducting in-depth research on the Internet. Students also link to a website called "School Town" to get a list of their daily "To Dos" programs. Starting in the sixth grade, all students receive their own Mac Book laptops to use for class activities and assignments.

Technology becomes a natural part of each student's development at Sacred Heart. However, the use of technology is not limited to the students. Sacred Heart also uses PowerSchool software which enables parents to obtain real-time information on their child's progress by subject. Parents can check on their child's homework assignments, test scores, and overall class grades. Thus, this technology helps to open up the dialogue among parents, students, and teachers.

THE TECHNOLOGY JOURNEY AT SACRED HEART SCHOOL

The Technology Specialist

Mrs. Sullivan, the current technology coordinator at Sacred Heart, was a regular classroom teacher who was always interested in technology, informed about its implementation, and knowledgeable of the relevant research. She became the technology coordinator at Sacred Heart several years ago. The principal, Sister Kathleen Donnelly, knew she was the perfect candidate, owing to her understanding of the school community, curriculum, technology, and how to bring it all together. Mrs. Sullivan helped implement the vision and a plan to bring Sacred Heart into the forefront of 21st-century advancements and was committed to working toward that purpose.

Mrs. Sullivan knew how important it was to include the entire faculty and staff in putting the technology plan into action, regardless of individua staff members' level of technological expertise. Mrs. Sullivan realized that because of her experiences as a classroom teacher she was better able to assist teachers and staff in taking what they knew about children, teaching, and learning and applying that knowledge to better integrate technology into the curriculum. Mrs. Sullivan explained, "Technology-infused lessons can best benefit the educational community if everyone, teachers and students, are involved." So although Mrs. Sullivan was charged as the "technology leader," decisions regarding technology were designed to impact as many members as possible.

In discussing technology and literacy, Mrs. Sullivan observes that focusing technology applications on reading and writing automatically engages students in all areas of the curriculum. Mrs. Sullivan's' experiences with teaching literacy in her own classroom helped her understand how important it was to motivate and engage students, a goal that can be much-enhanced by using technology. She also understands the use of varied audiences for both reading and writing while using technology. This awareness encourages her to help students be the best readers and writers they can be. As Mrs. Sullivan points out, "Students love to create and change. They approach everything as if it were a revisable script. They play to different audiences and begin to understand the importance of audiences in their writing." Reflecting back to her reading and writing classroom lesssons. Mrs. Sullivan adds, "The students used to write a paper for an audience of one (the teacher—me), but today they produce a living document in the form of a multimedia project. This allows their thoughts and creativity to live on in a more valuable way for a future audience of many. This enhances their level of ownership and 'buy in' to their own learning."

Mrs. Sullivan is dedicated to ensuring success for those who struggle with literacy. She observes that those who struggle as learners seem to "understand it better" when technology is integrated appropriately into literacy and the curriculum. The students realize there are technological tools that can assist their learning and understanding, and with that understanding they appear to be more engaged in their work and motivated to succeed.

Creating a Learning Environment That Incorporates Technology

At Sacred Heart, students are part of a learning environment where they are challenged to make the most of their cognitive skills and constantly prepare for the next level of academic achievement. This perspective informs Mrs. Sullivan's vision of technology implementation for the school. "We work to create an intimate learning environment where each child's learning style is taken into account," she notes, adding, "We live in an increasingly technology-driven world, so it is crucial that our students are proficient with the tools that will play an increasing role in their lives." To this end, technology is integrated into the curriculum in several ways at Sacred Heart so that students naturally learn to use it appropriately and productively. Each classroom has iMac computers to assist in the delivery of in-class programs and lessons. Multimedia SMART boards help teachers make class lessons interactive and dynamic. The SMART board technology also allows teachers to use the technology to teach, record, and replay lessons to their students.

Technology opens the doors for literacy learning especially for those who struggle. Text passages can be read aloud; grammar, spelling, and reference assistance is available; and writing can be dictated instead of typed. These are just a few of the "doors" that help with literacy in a learning environment that incorporates technology.

Ongoing Professional Development

A critical component of the technology plan at Sacred Heart is ongoing professional development and support for teachers. The goal of staff development at Sacred Heart is to help the faculty become comfortable and proficient with the technology, better enabling them to create authentic learning opportunities for students (Gauthier et al., 2006–2007). Mrs. Sullivan believes that this transitional period of adjustment is critical when moving teachers and staff toward a technology rich environment. Mrs. Sullivan learns with her colleagues and constantly models "no fear of failure." Mrs. Sullivan isn't afraid to say she doesn't know the answer or to try to problem-solve in front of her colleagues. She notes, "Our kids come into school knowing so much more about technology, and they are not afraid of it." They don't fail at using technology, they just tend to be persistent when solving a problem. In fact, teachers and students should partner with one another when implementing technology and learn together (Rae & Pederson, 2007).

Of course, if technical problems that are daunting persist for too long, teachers will return to more traditional ways of teaching. Technology that is not easily accessed and implemented will not be used. Teachers must have a good rationale for using technology in the first place and should be involved from the start in developing projects that apply technology to student learning (Cradler, 1996). Teachers also must have continuing access to on-site technical support personnel who are responsible for serious troubleshooting and assistance once the technology and lessons are in place.

Because they have the necessary support, teachers at Sacred Heart School are incorporating electronic whiteboard projects into their curriculum more and more each day. With this advancement, teachers are finding students more excited about learning and more involved with the curriculum, while teachers themselves are also excited by and involved with their increased knowledge of technology and its implications for better education.

RESEARCH ON NEW LITERACIES AND READING INSTRUCTION

Today, reading and reading instruction are being defined by change as new technologies require new literacies to effectively help all children read better and maximize their knowledge (Coiro, 2003; Kinzer & Leander, 2003; Lankshear & Knobel, 2003; Leu & Kinzer, 2000; Smolin & Lawless, 2003). Such technologies include electronic whiteboards, video editing and simulation techniques (O'Brien, 2001), improved search engines (Jansen, Spink, & Saracevic, 2000), simplified web hosting capabilities, with countless more advances to come. In addition, computer-based reading programs offer a wide variety of new literacies that continue to evolve rapidly. More importantly, new literacies can affect literacy instruction in classrooms, and educators need to stay informed (Hagood, Stevens, & Reinking, 2003, Lankshear & Knobel, 2003; Lewis & Finders, 2002).

Leu et al. (2004) agree that a definition of new literacies is difficult to determine because of rapid change in technology. However, Miners and Pascopella (2007) catalog some of the new literacies related to reading as social networking, e-mail, and instant messaging along with the Internet more broadly and other information and communication technologies (ICTs). These new literacies require students to both read and navigate electronically to locate information in addition to evaluating and using it effectively (Leu et al., 2007; Miners & Pascopella, 2007).

Teachers readily realize that no single teaching method reaches all students. Through use of technology and the new literacies that are increasingly woven into the curriculum, teachers can differentiate their instruction, providing content that is appropriately adapted to a wide range of students in each classroom. Integrating technology into the curriculum enables teachers to differentiate instruction by process (i.e., making sense of information) and the product (i.e., expressing what students learn) (Tomlinson, 1999). Students have many opportunities and choices when using technology. They can work alone or collaboratively, use auditory and/or visual modes, work on projects that interest them, and choose games that help them learn. Students who struggle the most with traditional literacy often appear to be highly engaged and motivated when using the new literacies (Miners & Pascopella, 2007). Educators and literacy leaders must themselves become more technologically literate at a much-accelerated pace and learn how to use extensive ICTs that become available in the new online networked environment.

Only when these new literacies are more fully integrated into the classroom environment will the needed reading support for *all* learners be a tangible reality (Gauthier et al., 2006–2007).

Once the Internet and other ICTs are firmly established in school classrooms, the central role of the teacher becomes one of orchestrating students' learning and literacy experiences, aided by technology. The teacher thoughtfully guides students' literacy progress by judiciously integrating technological aids in the service of the real-life concerns of the classroom. Although teachers are not necessarily technology experts, their key role is to assure that students ultimately are helped, not hindered, by the new technologies.

CONNECTING TO LEARNING: STUDENT ENGAGEMENT
AT SACRED HEART SCHOOL

First Graders' Number Sentences and Handwriting

Deana, a 10-year veteran and first grade teacher at Sacred Heart, shared with her class, "Be thinking about numbers we can for use for our number work today." The students sat on the rug in the front of the room after transitioning to their math lesson. Teacher helpers passed out the interactive worksheets and 10 chips. The students listened intently to all of the teacher's instructions, which were delivered in a clear and concise manner, and sat ready for the whole-class lesson with their whiteboards divided into 10 squares and their red chips by their side.

Deana projected a large dice and number sentences such as "4 take away ____ = ____" on the electronic whiteboard. She said, "Who would like to come up and roll the dice? Come up and roll the dice so that we can figure out this number sentence." Children came up enthusiastically to roll the dice—touching the Smart Board activated the dice. Then the dice would show a number that fit into the number sentence, and Deana said, "If we take 1 away from 4, how many do we have left?" First, the children reread the number sentence on the Smart Board and then answered the question. Next, they used their counters to show the answer to the sentence, using the counters to help them figure out the answer. Deana observed carefully to make sure that all the children were doing the problems correctly. The immediate feedback for all the children helped to motivate them during the lesson. Finally, when each student went up to show the number on the whiteboard, all eyes were on the student.

When the math lesson was over, Deana used the Smart Board for D'Nealian handwriting practice. Deana projected the program on the Smart Board screen, and a few students went up the whiteboard screen to practice forming letters, following the outline provided with their fingers. When the students wrote the letter correctly, the color changed to green. Also, the students had an opportunity to see the letter in its correct form in green when they were finished tracing the letter. Deana and the other students observed carefully to monitor the correct formation of the letters.

Solvie (2001) investigated students' attitudes toward literacy lessons that were given while using electronic whiteboard technology. She found that the interactive whiteboard created enthusiasm for learning on the part of the students, as evidenced by remarks made during the lessons presented using the Smart Board and during individual student interviews. Students remarked, "I like touching the Smart Board; my finger is magic. I like when the lines get different. It's a lot more easy using the interactive whiteboard, but I don't know why. The board is magic." Students were most engaged and interested when they actually touched the Smart Board or manipulated text on it.

All of the first graders in Deana's classroom were motivated throughout the math lesson and the handwriting lesson, with 100% participation. The lesson involving the interactive whiteboard also allowed for more interaction among the students, the learning materials, and the teacher. The whiteboard provided a large enough display surface for hands-on multimedia work, and having a large whiteboard surface encourages a high level of student interaction. The students listened to the teacher's spoken instructions, paid close attention to the math number sentences projected on the SMART board, and watched enthusiastically as their peers modeled how to form the letters.

Designing Study Webs in the Science Curriculum

Back in Emily Fogarty's fourth-grade classroom, students are busy cutting and pasting in their science notebooks in preparation for a whole-class lesson on creating study webs for a lesson on the topic "Five-Kingdom Classification System." Students are sitting in pairs but working individually to complete their preparations. While they are working, projected on the Smart Board is a stopwatch from *www.online.stopwatch.com*. The stopwatch does not interfere with the students' attention; they check it occasionally to make sure they finish their preparations on time. Emily suggests," If you are done before the rest of us, please get a book to read quietly while we finish cutting and pasting in our notebooks."

Emily begins with a short mini-lesson using the Smart Board. The students are instructed to circle three characteristics from the information on the "Five-Kingdom Classification System" that are the most interesting to them. An example from the plant kingdom is included in Figure 7.1.

All of the information on the "Five-Kingdom Classification System" was organized as the plant example. This was a challenging lesson with difficult vocabulary. However, all children in this classroom were engaged, reading, and motivated to complete developing their websites. They were designing the websites in teams on their computers.

Gerard and Widener (1999) note that when working with interactive whiteboards students generally appear to stay on task and are not distracted because the teacher can visually highlight important concepts. After the whole-group lesson, it was time to pass out the laptop computers so that students could share and collaborate while creating their team websites. With the computers turned on and ready, Mrs. Fogarty used the Smart Board to demonstrate how the children were going to begin working on their

PLANTS

You might think that grass, roots, and moss don't have much in common, but they are all members of the plant kingdom. All plants share the following characteristics.

- All plants make their own food. They do this through a process called **photosynthesis** (foh-toh-SIN-this-sis). In photosynthesis, plants use the energy in sunlight to change water and carbon dioxide into a kind of sugar called **glucose** (GLOO-kose). Glucose is food for the plant.
- Plants do not move from place to place.
- All plants are made of many cells. A plant has different cells. Each kind of cell has a different function.
- A plant cell has a stiff outer covering called the **cell wall**.
- Plants take in carbon dioxide from the air and give off oxygen into the air.
- Most kinds of plants reproduce with seeds. The seeds are made by flowers in some plants and by cones in other plants. Ferns and mosses reproduce with spores.
- Many plants originally had to adapt themselves for living on land.

FIGURE 7.1. Information used by students in the interactive "Five-Kingdom Classification System" lesson.

webs. She wrote **Kingdoms** in the middle of the whiteboard and continued to model the web design until it included a circle in the middle and the "Five-Kingdom Classification System" (monerans, protists, fungi, plants, and animals) extending from the middle. Mrs. Fogarty explained that the students should add three characteristics that they wanted to remember from their original worksheets. For example, the **PLANTS** extension radiating from **Kingdoms** in the middle circle would include the three items listed in boldface type in Figure 7.1.

The students worked well in pairs, collaborating and sharing the computer. Before completing the lesson, the students were instructed to plug in their flash drives to save their work. Students who needed help were aided by other students, and everyone completed this task successfully.

In Mrs. Fogarty's class, all students were actively engaged in designing their own study graphic organizers to facilitate the retention of the challenging curriculum they were learning. Using the study web facilitated the students' effective retention and review of the information. Mrs. Fogarty believes that using technology in lessons like these helped the children break down the information so that, after the students read a text selection, this interactive session reinforced their learning and deepened their understanding.

Meaningful Engagement: The iPod Touch

Colleen O'Donnell's second-grade students were working in groups, using playing cards to practice math facts. Colleen requested that the cards be put away, and the students then prepared for a handwriting lesson using the iPod Touch. The iPod Touch (*www.apple.com/ipodtouch*) is a portable media player, personal digital assistant, and Wi-Fi mobile platform designed and marketed by Apple Computer. Sacred Heart School has 30 iPod Touch portable media players available to students. Colleen said, "Instead of using our workbooks today to practice handwriting, we are going to use the iPod Touch." A resounding "Yeah!" was heard from every corner of the room.

The students listened to Colleen's careful instructions on how to find and use the handwriting application ABC Tracer, which is a free application developed by Oncilla Technologies for use on the iPod and the iPhone (*itunes.apple.com/us/app/alphabet-tracing/id374493089?mt=8*). Its target demographic is young children, and its goal is to help students learn how to correctly write the letters of the alphabet and numbers.

First, the screen displays either a letter or number that must be traced with the child's finger. A label is included to indicate which way the finger should move in order to accurately trace the letter. Then, as the child's finger drags along the screen, a small train, worm, or truck follows it. When the child forms the letter correctly, there is immediate feedback with an icon that claps and cheers. The application shows green for the correct formation and red if the formation is incorrect. With a click the child can see how the letter is formed.

Soon all students in the class were engaged in using their iPod Touch ABC Tracer application. First, the students traced all the lower-case letters, then the upper-case letters, and finally they traced whole words. They worked at their own pace, and when some students were finished working on the application, they had an opportunity to choose other applications. Some of the applications they could choose from included Bayou Beats, Deep Typer, Flashcards, Kids Math, Kid Match, Kinder Counting Matches, Mathmagics, Math Drills, Spanish LE, Rush-Hour, Shape Builders, Times Tables, and U.S.A. Presidents. By having an ample choice of programs from which to select, all the students were able to use their time efficiently and enjoy the programs that most interested them. Thus, all the children in the classroom were engaged in learning every minute. In addition, Colleen mentioned that a process is in place to facilitate requests from teachers and students for iPod Touch applications that they think might be productive independent learning opportunities.

In Colleen O'Donnell's classroom the students focused, participated, and interacted with the technology. The students talked quietly among themselves as Colleen walked around observing. Except for comments that focused on "I did it," "I love this," "What letter are you on," and "I did it perfectly right," all the students were intently focused on practicing their letters by using the iPod Touch. There was 100% participation in this lesson. The learning was very enjoyable and interesting for the students, even those who were considered to be struggling learners.

At the end of the lesson, the students helped Colleen put the iPod Touch devices into the individual cases. The students were instructed to get out their books and begin reading while Colleen stored the devices for their next user. Perhaps because the students had such an enjoyable and active time during the morning's activities, they settled down and immediately began reading their books, some reading aloud, some whisper reading, and some using fingers to mark their place—but everyone was reading.

Colleen, a newcomer to Sacred Heart, said that her opportunities to attend Apple's one-to-one workshops during the preceding summer had helped her to feel more comfortable with technology in the classroom. She attended 15 hours of workshops, and the intensive one-to-one training helped her immensely. Ongoing professional development at Apple is an invaluable yearly membership bonus (*www.apple.com/education/resources*).

Using the Yahoo Kids Search Engine: Completing a Project during Creepy Crawly Scary Month

The second graders in Amanda Burns's class were in the computer lab working on a classroom project for October, which they dubbed Creepy Crawley Scary Month. The 20 second graders sat at their computers with headsets on while working on research projects using the Yahoo search engine. They were working on the assignment in Figure 7.2.

All second graders were actively engaged in this activity, looking up their information. The teacher walked around the computer lab, seeking to facilitate the students' learning and encouraging them to complete the task successfully. The ultimate goal was for each of the students to use his or her facts to develop a composition about the spider for a Creepy, Crawly, Scary Month research project.

Integrating SMART Boards into the Reading and Writing Curriculum

On another day, Colleen O'Donnell's class reviewed a story they read from *Time for Kids* that included a time capsule, and Colleen shared a story she wrote from grade school that

---

Spider Search

1. Click on the "Yahooligans!" link on the My School Notes page.
2. Find the "Search" box on the "Yahooligans" web page.
3. Type in your spider name. The spider you will be learning about is the _____ .
4. Hit the return button, and the computer will look for the spider.
5. Click on the Yahooligans! Animal Match. This will be at the top of the page.
6. Once the page on your spider loads, read the information.
7. Write down three interesting facts about your spider.

    Fact #1: _____

    Fact #2: _____

    Fact #3: _____

When you are finished writing the facts, raise your hand and your teacher will help print out a picture of your spider to staple to this page.

FIGURE 7.2. Sample instructions for using the Yahoo Kids search engine.

she would include in a personal time capsule. On the Smart Board, she shared a poem about her experiences when she was in grade school. She read the poem aloud while students followed along with their eyes, some of them mouthing the words silently as she read. They then read the poem together, with just the lines the students were reading showing as a result of the Smart Board technology.

Colleen told the students that some of the words they read together were difficult words, so they were going to go over them together. She asked the students to come up to the Smart Board and circle words that they thought were hard to read or understand.

The first student circled *ancient* and Colleen asked, "What does *ancient* mean?"

STUDENT 1: It is really old-fashioned.

STUDENT 2: My uncle buys old cars.

STUDENT 3: Expensive.

STUDENT 4: It is like something that is really an old treasure that is *really* old like ancient Greece and ancient Egypt.

COLLEEN: If something is *ancient*, it is something that is really old, like a treasure. So, it can be expensive, but it could also be something like your great, great grandmother's handwritten recipe for bread. It might be *ancient*, and it might be a treasure, but it wouldn't be expensive.

The lesson continued with Colleen asking other students to come and circle words that they thought were difficult. The students circled *planetarium* and *vintage*. The next part of the lesson involved going over some aspects of African American history.

Colleen asked the students if anyone could share what they knew about Martin Luther King, Jr. First, Martin Luther King's name was written on the Smart Board. Responses from the students included "He made things fair," "He made speeches," and "He was from the South." When it came time to discuss other famous African Americans, Colleen scrolled down the screen on the Smart Board to draw the students' attention to other famous African Americans such as Rosa Parks, Harriet Tubman, Jackie Robinson, and Louie Armstrong. For Louie Armstrong, Colleen played his music and asked the students to take a few minutes to listen to the music.

Throughout this whole-class lesson, the students listened intently as Colleen worked on the Smart Board. Glover, Miller, Averis, and Door (2005) found evidence that suggests students are aware of three key benefits of lessons taught with the aid of interactive whiteboards, namely: (1) rapid responses to interactive examples, thereby reinforcing the learning immediately; (2) brighter and clearer presentation of the material; and (3) stepped learning and the immediate ability to recall earlier material.

Ms. O'Donnell's lesson demonstrated all the benefits that Glover et al. (2005) suggest. The Smart Board provided clear presentation of the material and also helped the students focus on the vocabulary that was the focus of one part of her lesson. And all eyes had been riveted on the Smart Board when the students choral read the poem together.

At this point in the lesson a student arrived late to class, but Ms. O'Donnell wasn't worried about the missed content. Through use of the Notebook software, in conjunction with a computer and the interactive whiteboard, any teacher can simply save a copy of what a student misses for his or her later review.

THEMES AND PATTERNS EMERGE

Several themes and patterns emerge from how lessons are conducted at Sacred Heart. First, the teachers create lesson plans that feature authentic and productive uses of technology. The teachers' careful preparation, planning, and attention to detail are obvious in the various class sessions observed. Second, students are highly engaged in all the learning activities. Strong engagement of students and high motivation are evident—whether reading to find out information for the school's science website, working on individual iPod applications, practicing math number sentences, or reading to find out information. Students know and understand their teachers' expectations. Third, students work collaboratively in pairs or small groups to accomplish the assigned tasks. Fourth, support from the administration and the technology specialist helps to integrate the use of the technology within the classroom and, in doing so, makes the technology relatively invisible. Finally, supporting a culture of change in the school is key to success in integrating technology into the curriculum. The teachers use the technology to support meaningful, engaged learning for all the students.

Gerard and Widener (1999) report that the use of the interactive whiteboard helps teachers become more organized in their teaching. Certainly the teachers at Sacred Heart deliver instruction and use technology in an organized and purposeful way. The use of technology accommodates a variety of learning styles in the classroom, enhancing student's motivation, in turn enabling teachers to exhibit greater enthusiasm for learning because they can concentrate on teaching, knowing that students are listening more intently.

When integrating technology, students can listen more closely to the teacher because they don't have to worry about taking notes (the notes being downloadable).

Ayn, who observed in Sacred Heart's classrooms, is an education and reading specialist. She was especially impressed with the engagement shown by all students—including those considered at risk or struggling—during lessons that used technology. In a questionnaire developed and analyzed by Miller and Glover (2002), teachers who used technology reported that children readily distracted during other lessons appeared to pay closer attention for longer periods of time when using interactive whiteboards and other technology.

With the advent of "new" literacies, literacy leaders are preparing themselves and their schools for a new direction in teaching. Most students are more experienced in new literacies than their teachers, and no single person is literate in every technology. This development suggests that learning may elvolve in more socially constructive ways as students and teachers learn the technology together—and that students may actually transform the literacies they use must as they contribute their own multimedia offerings to the Internet (Coiro, 2003; Miners & Pascopella, 2007).

IMPLEMENTING KEY IDEAS

It is critical when implementing technology into an elementary school program that the school officials and faculty set goals to integrate technology authentically into the curriculum. Here are some ideas to consider in designing how technology might best be used in schools to engage and support the reading improvement of all learners. Consider ways to:

- Create a culture of change in the school.
- Create a formal technology plan with the entire faculty's direct input.
- Develop proficiency in applying new technology innovations to the school environment through ongoing professional development.
- Create lesson plans that include authentic and productive uses of technology.
- Integrate appropriate technology into curricular areas.
- Review and update the technology plan on an ongoing basis and provide continual evaluation of its usefulness.
- Consider budgetary constraints in your planning, but also be alert to new funding possibilities.
- Schedule ongoing weekly meetings in which teachers have opportunities to share what is and isn't working.
- Provide parents with ongoing communications relating to the new literacies and curriculum goals.

CONCLUDING THOUGHTS

Technology in the school classrooms will increase, not decrease, the central role that teachers play in developing learning experiences for all students. Teachers will need to consider how to teach within these new information environments that are richer and more complex than traditional print media. The role of the teacher is crucial in choosing authentic meaningful lessons to engage and support all readers successfully.

CHAPTER EIGHT

Connecting with the Community

A suburban community known for its large size, Kiwald is both rural and urban. It boasts a bustling downtown as well as a rich agricultural area growing hay, wheat, walnuts, and tomatoes. The population is blue-collar, diverse, and in some areas transient. The school district of Kiwald encompasses a total of three towns in addition to the surrounding unincorporated areas. With 31 elementary schools, the district is one of the largest districts in the state.

Hyun-Yi, a credentialed reading specialist, worked as a kindergarten teacher in a neighborhood that provided accommodations for low-income families who frequently moved to find work. The school was classified as Title I (under ESEA), with 60% of the students receiving free or reduced breakfast and lunch. There were a high number of low-performing students who were not able to achieve the academic standards set forth by the state, and the teachers, though trying hard to help their students, were disheartened that their efforts did not always produce positive results.

Hyun-Yi was also disheartened but refused to be discouraged. She was determined to prepare her emergent readers and writers to succeed not only in kindergarten but in subsequent years. During this particular year, 73% of her families spoke English as their second language, with 66% being Hispanic or Latino. It was this year that she decided to enlist the parents as partners in helping their children to achieve.

This chapter explores the efforts first of a teacher and then of a school community to connect with students, parents, and the larger community to create literacy partnerships that are mutually beneficial. Research-based suggestions are provided to build these connections, followed by ideas for implementation. Hyun-Yi continues by explaining why she struggled with the prospect of viable partnerships with the parents of her students.

"I knew that children's literacy experiences at home influenced their success in school," noted Hyun-Yi, "but that cultural, social, and economic factors were also influences. With low-income multiethnic families, my goal was to help the families create a rich family literacy environment in their homes, but I knew it wasn't going to be easy! Our parents don't come to school" (Goldenberg, 2008; Whitehurst & Lonigan, 1998).

The school had tried a number of activities and programs to create home–school connections, but none was very successful. Hyun-Yi decided to start out small in the hope that the family literacy program she developed would eventually include all grades in the school. "Sometimes you need to start with baby steps," she explained. "We started with just my morning and afternoon kindergarten families as a kind of pilot program to see what worked and how we could create a family-friendly atmosphere."

STARTING SMALL WITH A BIG PLAN

Hyun-Yi began by reading and researching. She wanted to know what researchers had found successful and the variety of obstacles she would need to overcome. Armed with knowledge, Hyun-Yi designed a research-based plan of action whose elements were (1) survey the parents and guardians to determine what types of literacy activities were already present in the homes of her students; (2) survey the parents and guardians to learn what the most convenient times to offer activities at school were for them; (3) assess the students to learn their greatest strengths and challenges, to determine what should be addressed in the workshops; (4) plan interactive workshops to be held every 2 weeks, with alternative dates and formats for those unable to attend; (5) subsequently survey the parents and guardians to learn why (if so) they were unable to attend, and (6) survey the parents and guardians to determine what they found to be the most useful information disseminated in the workshops.

While planning, Hyun-Yi also had to consider how to pay for this undertaking. The school district was willing to fund the costs of copying the parent materials, and she decided to pay for the refreshments herself. If the workshops were successful enough to continue beyond the current year, she would ask the principal for a small budget to cover some of the costs. She would also seek financial and volunteer assistance from the local Parent Teacher Association (PTA) and the donation of supplies and other materials from local businesses. There were a few families in the district who owned restaurants, and she could entice them with free publicity if they donated snacks. Finally, an interested room parent could be tapped to coordinate a treat schedule for the instructional events.

Surveying Parents and Guardians before the Workshops

Hyun-Yi wanted to build on what was already happening outside of school; so, she needed to know if reading was already taking place in the homes of her students. She developed a survey in English and Spanish that would help her determine the literacy topics she might include in the workshops, based on the children's reading frequency in the home. Trying to keep the survey simple and inviting, she asked:

1. How many days during the week, if any, did an adult read to the kindergartener?
2. How many days during the week, if any, did the kindergartener read to an adult?
3. How many days in the week, if any, did an adult assist with kindergarten writing activities at home?
4. How many days during the week, if any, did the kindergartener engage with books or stories of any kind? (This last question was included to honor oral story telling or other culturally based reading practices.)

After assessing the resulting survey data, Hyun-Yi concluded that literacy activities were transpiring in homes an average of 2 days a week. Her plan's goal was simply to *increase* that frequency.

Two weeks later, a second survey was sent home; also translated into Spanish, it related to workshop scheduling. Hyun-Yi had already decided that she would offer workshops with alternative dates and formats, but she needed to know when most families were available to come to the school. The survey shown in Figure 8.1 was sent via the child to all students' homes and followed up by phone calls to families who did not return the form within 2 weeks.

Dear Parents and Guardians,

As you already know, I am planning workshops to share literacy activities you can do with your child at home. Before I set the dates and times, I need to know when it would be most convenient for you to attend. Please fill out the grid below and return it in the Take Home folder of your child. If you have any questions about literacy or topics you want me to address, please add those as well. Thank you! I appreciate your response.

Put an *X* in the box if you or members of your family are able to come to school for a workshop during that time and day:

	Monday	Tuesday	Wednesday	Thursday	Friday
3:00–4:00					
4:00–5:00					
5:00–6:00					
7:00–8:00					

Add any literacy questions or topics you would like me to discuss below.

FIGURE 8.1. Survey to determine when most families would be able to attend a literacy workshop.

Assessing Students

A battery of emergent and early literacy assessments had already been developed for kindergarteners at the school. Hyun-Yi administered these assessments in October not only to inform her instruction but also to determine the areas where parents could assist in meeting students' needs. These standardized assessments were administered in both whole-class settings and one-on-one. The assessments included:

- Naming upper- and lower-case letters.
- Producing consonant and short-vowel sounds.
- Blending and segmenting words for phonemic awareness.
- Reading high-frequency words.
- Blending consonant–vowel–consonant words.
- Rhyming.
- Understanding print concepts.

Developing the Workshops

Hyun-Yi was determined to create a family literacy program that parents would want to attend to learn how to help their children. She knew that the program's success—and thus ultimately the student's progress—would depend on the parents' attendance. Therefore, to resolve the problem of convenience, the workshops were scheduled every 2 weeks from November to January. Each 1-hour workshop was offered after school and then repeated in the evening to maximize parents' participation. The kindergarteners were also urged to attend, and other children in the family were welcome if child care was an issue!

The workshops all followed the same agenda so that families would feel comfortable knowing the sequence of events. After 10 minutes for refreshments and conversation, the workshop formally began with a sing-along and a game, followed by a demonstration of an early literacy concept with a related activity and another game. Parents practiced the demonstrated activity with their child while Hyun-Yi walked around to help and to answer questions. The workshop concluded with a song and encouragement to read and practice at home what the audience had learned at the workshop. Parents were also asked to fill out an evaluation of the workshop session immediately afterward each time.

Conferences were held for parents every 2 weeks, both for families who had been unable to attend the workshop earlier and for those who wanted any kind of additional help or information. The conferences were scheduled to be held between 11:30 A.M. and 12:30 P.M. so that working parents could possibly attend during their lunch break. It also was a convenient time for family caretakers such as grandparents, aunts, or uncles who came to school to pick up their kindergarteners and then could remain for a conference. Sometimes Hyun-Yi even persuaded parents who had never attended a workshop to come back to her classroom after picking up their child, and there she was able to share the workshop information.

The Workshop Content

With 10 minutes at the start and finish of the workshop for opening and closing activities, 40 minutes were left for the demonstrations, activities, and family practice. The literacy concepts demonstrated in the workshops focused, in order of coverage, on the alphabet; rhyming; letter–sound relationships; high-frequency words; how to choose good books; shared, echo, and partner reading; engaging the child's comprehension abilities; retelling of reading selections; developmental spelling (also known as invented spelling) and writing; and student-dictated stories. These concepts not only followed a developmental sequence, but also reflected much of what was taught in the classroom. In this way, the students received a "double dose" of learning—once at school and again at home.

The activities and games also followed a developmental sequence. The children had already played some of the literacy games at school, while others were new. This combination gave the children a sense of accomplishment for being able to show what they already knew (in the case of familiar games) but also to find a challenge (in the unfamiliar

TABLE 8.1. A Sample of Workshop Activities and Games

Title	Description
Alphabet flash cards	Provided with upper- and lower-case letters copied on card stock, families learned a number of sequencing, sorting, and matching games. Parents were given a listing of the alphabet letters their child knew and those they were still learning, and they were told to use a mixture of known and unknown letters in the games.
Letter and word fun with magnetic letters	A neighborhood store sold buckets of magnetic letters for $1; so, families learned the exercises in Making Words (Cunningham & Cunningham, 1992) that could be used with the magnetic letters or alphabet flash cards.
Word families and sorting	Families made two sets of six short consonant–vowel–consonant word cards for the word families of -at and -ap. These were used for sorting and games (Bear et al., 2007).
Echo reading	Parents learned how to point to each word while reading a single sentence to their child. Their child then "echoed" the same sentence back, pointing to each word as it was pronounced. The parent then pointed and read the next sentence, which was again echo read by the child.
Authentic writing	Families considered ways to bring more writing into the lives of their children. Letters, thank-you notes, grocery lists, e-mails, and Facebook and Twitter posts became part of the student's writing or dictation activities at home.

game). Table 8.1 lists some of the activities and games families played together during the workshops.

Both the parents and the children found the practice time enjoyable. The room was filled with smiling families huddled together, laughing and playing. This reaction was what Hyun-Yi had hoped for because she knew that if the families had a good time they were more likely to continue the games at home and attend future workshops.

Book Bags

Another way to help families engage with the reading strategies they were learning was to loan them book bags for their use at home. These book bags contained books for both the students and adults to read aloud, books on CDs, children's songs and nursery rhymes on CDs and DVDs, and a list of the items included so that nothing would be forgotten when the bag was returned. Each bag also included a reading log (see Figure 8.2 for a sample) so that parents could not only monitor the amount of time they engaged in literacy activities with their child but also could write their responses to the activities (at the bottom of the form). Parents were not always sure how to respond to the literacy activities; so, guiding questions were provided in each book bag, namely:

- "What was the family's favorite book or reading activity?"
- "What were some of the words you knew how to read?"
- "What were some of the hard words you were learning to read?"
- "What did you learn?"
- "Did any of the stories remind you of something that happened to your family or to you?"
- "Which stories made you feel scared, happy, silly, confused, or sad?"
- "What 'I wonder ... ' thoughts did you have?"

Families were encouraged to record their responses in any language they wanted, and—with this freedom—most did respond.

Book bags were loaned to families for a week. There was a check-out system that also enabled Hyun-Yi to know which book bags had been home with each family. Because she was working with two classes of families, Hyun-Yi did not have enough book bags to give one to every family each week. To supplement the bags, she encouraged families to go on the Internet to sites such as those listed in Table 8.2 to find online read-aloud books or texts. Families without computers at home were encouraged to use the computers available in the school or at the local public library.

Family Attendance

Although many families attended the workshops, Hyun-Yi wanted full participation. She needed to understand the reasons that families were unable to attend—not only so that

Weekly Reading Log for _____

Family name: _____

Week of: _____

Mark how often you read each day by placing an X in the correct column.

	We read less than 20 minutes.	We read for about 20 minutes.	We read more than 20 minutes.
Sunday			
Monday			
Tuesday			
Wednesday			
Thursday			
Friday			
Saturday			
Please respond to your book bag activities.			

FIGURE 8.2. Book bag reading log.

TABLE 8.2. Websites That Feature Read-Aloud Books or Texts

Website	Highlights
www.storylineonline.net	Well-known picture books are introduced and read aloud, with captions, by members of the Screen Actors Guild.
www.magickeys.com/books	Of the many selections, only a few have audio for a read-aloud. The site includes links to phonics games.
www.speakaboos.com	A wide variety of stories, including multicultural selections, are read in English. The site includes songs and information for parents.
www.pbskids.org/lions/stories	Folktales and fables are shared from the Public Broadcasting System (PBS) program *Between the Lions*. Words and phrases are highlighted while being read aloud.
www.storyplace.org	Stories at the preschool level include songs with text available in Spanish and English.

she could try to accommodate them better but also to plan for family literacy workshops in the future. She created a survey (see Figure 8.3) to determine the barriers to attendance and had it translated into Spanish.

The data showed that most parents didn't attend her workshops because they already felt comfortable with their own ways of helping their child with reading at home. This response made sense because many kindergarteners had older siblings who had already been through kindergarten. Work obligations were cited as the second most common reason for not attending, followed by exhaustion and problems arranging for child care.

Hyun-Yi took due note of the barriers and tried to think of new ways of reaching all the parents. She planned to add workshop topics like "Reading and Recipes" or "Using

Have you ever missed a Family Literacy Workshop? I'd like to understand why so that I can help everyone have the opportunity to attend. Please check all reasons that apply.

I missed the Family Literacy Workshop because:

_____ I do not have transportation.

_____ I work in the afternoons and evenings.

_____ I am too tired in the afternoons and evenings.

_____ I cannot find child care.

_____ I wasn't aware of the Family Literacy Workshops.

_____ I am comfortable helping my child at home and do not need to attend.

Please write any reasons that were not mentioned above that also apply to you.

FIGURE 8.3. Barriers to family literacy participation.

Television Captions to Promote Reading" to entice those who already felt comfortable with their child's basic kindergarten literacy skills. She also planned to add morning conference times for those who worked in the afternoons, and she considered arranging to digitally record or videotape the workshop sessions so that those who could not attend might still be able to benefit.

Workshop Evaluations

Families evaluated the workshops immediately after each one ended and at the conclusion of the whole series. The evaluations after each session enabled Hyun-Yi to make improvements in her later workshops (see Figure 8.4). In general, the parents' comments were very positive, and families were happy to have time to learn together.

As the workshop sessions ended, Hyun-Yi wanted to know what parents and guardians found to be the most and least helpful information and activities. Parents generally noted that the activities and games with high-frequency words were most helpful. They appreciated that the materials were given to them at the workshop so they could go home and use them immediately. They found the information on print concepts least helpful; so, Hyun-Yi said she would rethink the content and presentation style of that particular workshop.

As the workshops and school year drew to a close, Hyun-Yi also wondered what she should change to improve her relationships with parents. Another remaining concern was how to involve other grade levels so that eventually there would be a rich and fruitful connection with the families schoolwide.

Such a rich and fruitful connection was evident at Mimosa Park Elementary School, which we describe next.

A SCHOOL'S FOCUS ON COMMUNITY CONNECTIONS

The faculty and staff at Mimosa Park Elementary School (MPE) in Luling, Louisiana, also know how important it is to maintain close relations with their students' families. Luling, a picturesque town perched on the banks of the Mississippi River some 20 miles upriver from New Orleans, is part of the St. Charles Parish Public School District. St. Charles Parish has an illustrious history of thriving antebellum plantations that once grew vegetables, rice, and sugar cane and then became a center of industry (Wilson, 1976). Currently the population of Luling is increasing as more families move to the town (*www.stcharles.k12.la.us*), and Mimosa Park Elementary School has many more students than it was originally built to accommodate. New schools are under construction in the community.

Michele, Mimosa Park's principal, feels very strongly about literacy. The school was awarded the International Reading Association's Exemplary Reading Program Award in 2010 for its outstanding work with literacy that included partnering with families and

Workshop Evaluation

Date: _____   Session: Afternoon   Evening

Please comment, and leave this evaluation form on the table before you leave. Thank you. Your comments will help to improve the sessions.

1. Did this session meet your expectations?   Yes   No

2. What could be done to improve the session? _____

   _____

   _____

   _____

3. Was there enough time to cover the topics?   Yes   No

   Any suggestions for improvements? _____

   _____

   _____

   _____

4. Was the information presented in a clear and understandable manner?   Yes   No

5. How will you use the materials you received?

   _____

   _____

   _____

   _____

6. Please offer any suggestions or comments.

   _____

   _____

   _____

   _____

   _____

   _____

FIGURE 8.4. Workshop evaluation form.

the community. Under Michele's guidance, the administrators, faculty, and staff have developed a model partnership with parents that involves the hard work of all faculty and staff members.

Mimosa Park's vision statement explicitly includes parents and the community as being important in the education of the first- through third-grade children that the school serves. To start each academic year, school community builds strong relationships with parents during the Back to School Bash, which takes place the day before school officially begins.

The Back to School Bash is held on the school grounds from 1:30 to 3:30 P.M., with some 90% of the families attending an open house of sorts that captures the atmosphere of a grand festival. The first stop for most families is the children's classrooms, where their parents meet their new teachers, fill out any necessary forms, and receive a token of welcome. After that, they are offered a variety of services to help with numerous special needs:

- Enrichment teachers are available to meet parents and children and talk about their programs.
- Bus drivers meet the families and children that will commute with them each morning and afternoon.
- A public librarian takes applications for library cards while the school librarian awards medals to students who successfully accomplished 1,000 minutes of summer reading in the school's reading incentive program.
- Boy and Girl Scout troop and Parent Teacher Organization representatives receive applications.
- School fundraiser committee members distribute flyers on their upcoming projects.
- A community hospital representative answers questions.
- The fire department and police department are on hand to record new enrollees' fingerprints.
- The Regional Transportation Authority (RTA) registers parents for their services. If a parent lacks convenient transportation to the school for conferences or other school activities, a reservation can be made with the RTA 24 hours in advance, and a bus will transport the parent for a cost of only $2.
- The principal, Michele, welcomes everyone back to school.
- There is enough jambalaya for everyone to enjoy!

The Back to School Bash is a popular occasion for community members to come together to support one another, build relationships, and renew ties. Every year this gathering gets larger, and it is a highly anticipated event for all involved. And while the Back to School Bash sets the tone for this annual renewal of community connections, special activities in the area of literacy can allow for school officials' partnering with parents and guardians as well.

Parent Open House

The Mimosa Park Parent Open House begins much like a typical school open house, with a half-hour in the child's classroom spent reviewing important information, routines, and procedures for the year. For the next hour, however, parents attend half-hour sessions of parent education. These sessions present literacy and math materials and strategies, writing organizational skills, and information about assessment and the child's report card.

Literacy, Math, and Science Nights

During the month of November, each grade-level team of teachers hosts its own special open house. In the first grade the theme is always literacy; in the second grade it is math; and in third grade, science. Parents and guardians attend with their children on the designated night for an hour of activities, informative pursuits, and delightful treats.

On Literacy Night, the first-grade team of teachers creates several self-directed stations that offer useful materials on reading, writing, word study, and multisensory ways to connect to books. The first graders share what they are learning, and the parents find out how they can assist them at home. Because the first-grade teachers always manage to arrange an exciting and motivating evening, the event is always well attended.

On later November weeknights, the second- and third-grade teachers host their special nights. Organized in a similar fashion, the second graders' Math Night focuses on problem solving, while the third graders' Science Night highlights experiments. Middle schoolers visit Science Night to share their experiences in Wetland Watchers, a nationally known organization created to save the wetlands, bringing with them some 20–25 animals featured in a discussion on animal care and endangered species.

Parents as Partners

Parents and guardians are invited to join the teachers in assisting the students. Those who wish to volunteer and make a firm commitment to work regularly with the children are subsequently trained in literacy and math strategies. The training initially occurs toward the beginning of the school year and continues throughout the academic year. A parent assisting with literacy might, for example, visit one classroom twice a week to assist a group of four first graders with rereading for fluency and word recognition for a half-hour, then work one-on-one with another student who needs help with comprehension strategies, and finally facilitate a literature circle discussion with second graders. Parents come to realize that they can also use the strategies learned in their volunteer work at home to assist their own children.

Connecting with Parents

With the understanding that parents need to be comfortable with the school as well as be aware of what is happening there, the faculty and staff at Mimosa Park communicate with parents as much as possible. To begin, each teacher has a website for parents and students (see *www.stcharles.k12.la.us/classroompages.cfm?location=8*) that includes a variety of information such as homework news, contact information, and a calendar of events.

Newsletters from Mimosa Park are sent home monthly (see the MPE newsletter at *www.stcharles.k12.la.us/mimosa.cfm*) while parent information sheets from individual teachers are sent home weekly. These sheets include important updates, homework, curricular objectives, and any other communication related to the week's events. The Parent Teacher Organization is strong at Mimosa Park and committed to getting parents involved. They also communicate with parents on behalf of the school through phone calls and e-mails.

Special consideration is given to families considered at risk to make them feel welcome and part of the school community. Faculty and staff members contact parents, guardians, and students frequently to offer invitations to events, help with resources, and just touch base. While some parents might be inclined to shy away from school events, with the stepped-up personal contact many feel a special connection to the school. This enhanced personal and community connection is evident even in the web pages posted on the school's website. Along with suggestions for children, the website includes recommendations for careers, computer information, and government services (see *www.stcharles.k12.la.us/mimosa.cfm?subpage=63&schoolNav*).

Perci's Pelican Prize Patrol

While not directly connected to literacy, a unique outreach program is nonetheless worth mentioning. Mimosa Park's spring outreach event builds on the school's special relationships with families and recognizes students for their hard work and good character. In the spirit of the Publishers Clearing House prize patrol, a busload of faculty and staff members visit 15 student residences on four separate weekdays after school hours. The students are randomly selected from a pool of candidates based on teacher recommendations for "great character all year long." Parents are notified ahead of time; so, when there is a knock at the door, the student opens it to Perci Pelican, the school's mascot; a group of cheering adults; a balloon bouquet; and principal Michele with an award of recognition, a $20 gift certificate to either a bookstore or the Scholastic Book Club.

Perci's Pelican Prize Patrol members are usually welcomed into the students' homes and invited to stay for a buffet of food, short recitals, or just a big hug from everyone. Michele explains: "We celebrate as one community during Perci's Pelican Prize Patrol. We show that we are there for the families, but we need them to be there for us too.

When we come to their homes, families feel more comfortable coming to school and helping us support their children" (personal communication, September 22, 2010).

BUILDING PRODUCTIVE PARTNERSHIPS

A partnership is a relationship in which responsibility is shared through mutual understanding and collaborative actions. In a partnership, literacy leaders need to nurture established and growing relationships to involve families in supporting literacy growth. In this section, we examine research that corroborates that the partnerships described in this chapter provide guidance and sustenance in helping to build stronger community connections.

Start with the Family

Although school is an institution for learning, a great deal of learning takes place at home as well. Parents are important teachers who have a significant influence on their children's education (Padak & Rasinski, 2007). Children and young adults are influenced by what happens at home, and this influence is reflected in their motivation, self-confidence, and attitudes (Hersch, 1998–1999; Rogoff, 1990; Steward, Golf, & Harris, 2007).

Hyun-Yi (whom we discussed earlier in this chapter) solicited parents' input first before organizing her workshops. She asked about literacy in homes and parents' schedules. She encouraged parents to evaluate her workshops and kept in touch with the students' families to ensure their year-round participation. Both the families and teachers benefited from the partnership in the form of literacy progress.

In a not totally dissimilar fashion, Mimosa Park Elementary starts every school year with a much-celebrated "Bash" for families. In other words, the school begins building its relationships with families immediately by welcoming them with open arms and trying to meet their needs as best it can (Risko & Walker-Dalhouse, 2009). With so many families attending the "Bash," it is the perfect time to begin or renew the school's "mutually beneficial partnerships" (p. 442) with families.

Literacy leaders are wise to partner with parents and guardians—especially so, given the parents' uniquely intimate knowledge of their own children. Penny, the parent of a middle schooler, was thrilled when, during the first week of school, her son's teacher asked parents and guardians to answer a few questions about their soon-to-be teenagers.

> "I love the fact that the teacher wanted to get to know my son on a personal
> level. Not every child fits into that perfect little box, and as a teacher, it some-
> times requires thinking outside the box to adapt to other children's learning

styles. My son is not a nondescript 11-year-old boy that she learned about in a book. He is an individual with unique learning styles, quirks, and interests, and is different from the child that is sitting beside him. It takes a special teacher to understand this and, even more importantly, to want to learn about each child in order to establish a working relationship with the parent or guardian for the best interest of the student."

From that point on, Penny regarded her relationship with the teacher as a partnership with shared responsibility for the growth of her son, and her son benefited immensely as a result. "I think it's fine that they talk to each other, especially when it helps with my homework," Penny's son, Zac, admitted, quickly adding, "as long as I don't have to be there when they are talking!"

Connect for Authentic Purposes

At times, Zac struggled with his homework; so, the partnership between his parents and teacher was highly purposeful (Rasinski & Padak, 2009). The teacher knew that connecting with parents based on students' individual strengths and challenges would be an authentic reason for working together. Hyun-Yi and the Mimosa Park Elementary School teachers connected with parents based on the genuine needs of the students and the community to create a rich environment for all, regardless of income level, language, or ethnicity.

See the Power in Diversity

We are all unique. Life experiences, cultures, similarities, and the differences in people create strengths that can be beneficial for students and teachers. When parents and teachers come together in a respectful way, these personal strengths can foster innovation, flexibility, efficiency, and creativity. The potential for everyone to benefit is immense, and establishing practices and procedures to involve parents and community members in worthwhile endeavors should always be a key goal (Elish-Piper, 2008; Morrow, 2009).

Realize That Parents Care

We both had experiences while we were teaching when it appeared that parents simply didn't care about either their child or the school. In every case, the parent did indeed care, but such interfering factors as multiple jobs, having to attend night school, or their limited understanding of English made it hard for the parents to stay connected (Elish-Piper, 2008). All efforts made by teachers and staff to connect with parents go a long way, and the parents usually end up reciprocating by also making the effort to stay connected because they eventually come to realize how much they are supported by the school (Morrow, 2009).

Make It Fun

Of course, it can't be done in every circumstance, but *whenever possible* strive to create a productive and enjoyable atmosphere for partnering and connecting. Sharing food, stories, writing, and literacy activities creates sustained partnerships and community connections. Parents will be glad to work with the school community when they see that—at least some of the time—there will be fun, engaging experiences to benefit all.

IMPLEMENTING KEY IDEAS

Initially time and effort are needed to develop long-lasting partnerships and community connections, but this obstacle shouldn't deter literacy leaders from creating these associations. With partnerships comes joint responsibility, which suggests that both educators and community members must ultimately supply the needed time and effort to get the job done properly. Here are some basic suggestions for getting started:

- Develop a newsletter or website that can be shared widely with both parents and the local community. When students engage in particularly exemplary or unique literacy activities, invite the local press to cover the "news."
- Start with just one partnering project, understanding that participation will grow as community members and parents see the value of the project's content and the centrality of the school–home relationship.
- Learn as much as you can about the members of the community. Send out surveys and talk with parents to closely assess their most deeply felt needs so that partnering projects can be designed or shaped to meet those needs to the utmost.
- Consider the budgetary constraints in place, but also be alert to potential new funding possibilities.
- Arrange to hold partnering meetings, workshops, or events at convenient times or be willing to repeat the sessions to achieve optimal attendance results.
- Help arrange car pools or a method of transportation for those who need it. Consider the parking options when multiple grade levels sponsor a partnering project at the same time.
- Consider partnering sessions with literacy topics for adults only and provide convenient child care for them. With the supervision of a few adults, Girl Scouts and Boy Scouts can provide child care while parents attend the session. Be sure to also offer sessions at alternative times that consider families' needs so all can better attend.
- Develop sessions with engaging interactive literacy content.
- Provide follow-up materials for participants in the form of conferences notes, summaries of the partnering session, and additional information.
- Ask participants to evaluate the partnering session or project. Analyze the data to improve future sessions.

CONCLUDING THOUGHTS

Connecting firmly with parents to create a solid ongoing partnership provides a framework for continuous improvement, personal growth, and greater achievement by students, one that could not be created if parents and schools worked alone. Because parents and teachers share the responsibility for learning, they then share the successes of the students. The advantages of connecting with parents are worth the time and effort expended, especially because it is the student who ultimately benefits the most!

CHAPTER NINE

Planning for a Literacy Leader's
First Professional Development Session

Success [in professional development] rests in finding the optimal
mix of process elements and technologies that then can be carefully,
sensibly, and thoroughly applied in a particular setting.
—THOMAS R. GUSKEY

Renee walked over to join a group of teachers in a bright, comfortable room. She was
confident as she addressed them. "Good morning," she said. "Many of you know me, but
for those of you who don't, my name is Renee. Over the next weeks we are going to spend
some time together thinking about writing fiction and teaching writing to the students in
your classrooms. We'll talk about minilessons, student-centered inquiry, apprenticeship,
and shared reading as they relate to writing fiction. First, however, I'd like you to share
with me what you want to learn or what you are trying to get out of these sessions."
Renee picked up a black marker and was ready to record the teachers' comments on the
whiteboard.

When Renee drove to meet the teachers that morning, she purposefully tried to
relax. It was the first day she would lead a professional development session in her new
position. Renee was a literacy leader and a classroom teacher, but she had just been hired
to be a teacher on special assignment who would meet with her colleagues throughout
the district to facilitate multiple professional development sessions and classroom support in the area of writing. "When I first started," Renee reflected, "I was nervous and
scared. I knew the material I was to going to cover well but, teaching *adults*?—that was
going to be quite different from teaching children! But, by supporting the classroom

teachers, the student writers in their classrooms would benefit, and that, for me, was the most important factor."

To help with the transition from teaching children to teaching adults full-time, Renee read books and journal articles, critiqued the professional development sessions of literacy experts she admired, and planned side by side with fellow literacy leaders from the district. She began working with teachers who taught in third through fifth grades, because those were the grade levels in which she felt most comfortable, but eventually she worked at all grade levels. Over this and subsequent years, she continued to learn how to better plan and organize her presentations, pace herself while demonstrating self-confidence, use support materials and props, and engage her audience.

This chapter is written for literacy leaders like Renee who, for the first time, must share their expertise with colleagues in the form of a professional development session. The chapter's inclusion in this volume and its specific organization are based on the advice and recommendations of newly credentialed reading specialists who were asked to present staff development sessions. They were eager to do well and to successfully implement change, knowing that students would ultimately benefit from their efforts.

PROFESSIONAL DEVELOPMENT FOR A NOVICE

Schools are always looking to stay within their budgets, especially during times of economic stress. Lately budgets have been dramatically cut, and literacy leaders have been called upon to implement more professional development because funding is no longer available to hire outside experts. In addition, exemplary models of professional development require long-term funding support that cannot be depended upon to finance one-time visits from consultants, but sometimes can provide for a school or district site literacy leader.

In this chapter, literacy leaders who have implemented professional development programs for their schools and districts, shared with us their considered reflections about how relatively inexperienced literacy leaders should approach the subjects of professional planning, implementation, and follow-up. They offer concrete suggestions and advice for those making a professional presentation for the very first time. In this chapter, this informed group of advisors are referred to as the Professional Development Literacy Leaders (PDLL).

Beginning with an overview of professional development, we proceed to examine in turn, adult learners, topic choice, and a needs assessment to guide planning. Next, the professional development environment, participant engagement, and session preparation are discussed at length, followed finally by comments on evaluations and how best to support short- and long-term change.

WHY PROFESSIONAL DEVELOPMENT IN LITERACY IS ESSENTIAL

Students are in school to learn. Gaskins (2005) describes learning as "a complex interactive process that requires the intent or goal to create meaning plus the mental activity to achieve the learning goal" (p. 150). Reading well can be a learning goal in and of itself—or reading can allow one *access* to a separate learning goal. For example, to achieve the goal of understanding the early settlement of Egypt, a sixth grader might be assigned to read *The History of the Ancient World,* a textbook. Being able to read well gives the student ready *access* to the relevant information on Egypt. How can schools be sure their students are able to meet the requisite academic standards—especially in reading? One key way is through teachers' adequate professional development.

Professional development is a series of activities intended to improve or enrich the "knowledge, skills, and attitudes" (Guskey, 2000, p. 16) of those who educate so that their students are better able to learn (Bean, 2009). The goal of professional development in education is to provide teachers (who ultimately are responsible for students' learning success) the experiences and tools to capably assist students and ensure their achievement. School officials provide for the professional development of the teachers, in effect, establishing a schoolwide learning community composed of the faculty and staff (Lyons & Pinnell, 2001).

When schools provide professional development, the teachers and administrators together can develop goals for both teachers' and students' learning based on local, professional, or state standards to provide high-quality instruction. A plan to provide support for administrators, teachers—and therefore students—based on learning goals can then be implemented, and educators can work collaboratively toward those goals (Bean, 2009; Lyons & Pinnell, 2001).

Any school that develops specifically defined goals to improve reading automatically involves the teachers in every content area and grade level, thereby requiring that all staff members, including administrators, thereafter work closely and contribute to ongoing conversations relating to future professional development and reading goals. These conversations, along with long-term professional development, over time enhance instruction across all the grade levels and lead to improved student reading schoolwide.

Schoolwide professional development in reading therefore is a worthy undertaking. And when the school community embraces the goal of improved reading, all significant stakeholders, including parents, should ideally share in the responsibility for attaining the goal (Reeves, 2006). For example, the principal should arrange for teachers to observe others' teaching methods in the classrooms of colleagues; individual teachers might demonstrate a reading strategy that they find particularly useful at staff meetings; and parents might volunteer to work with teachers and students—each initiative geared toward improving reading performance. In this fashion, the goal of improving reading becomes a truly schoolwide venture, with all those involved in the school working together toward, and sharing responsibility for, students' success.

BRIEF INTRODUCTION TO THE ADULT LEARNER

In this section, someone new to presentations intended for professional development can begin to better understand adult learners. A few important considerations must be kept in mind as one develops these activities, fully realizing that additional resources are readily available if further information is required. The following description is intended only as a brief overview.

Adults are very complicated learners. They are highly diverse in their prior knowledge and experiences, and the task of teaching an adult—whose life experiences remain largely unknown to any observer—can be challenging. On the other hand, diverse knowledge and experiences can enrich learning when new insights are blending with old to impact professional and personal lives. The most effective adult educators seek to match the unique characteristics of their adult students with the professional development tools and methods in their personal arsenal (Long, 2004).

Adults learn best when the information conveyed to them is meaningful and relevant to their personal or professional lives. When such information is meaningful, the topic or innovation commands one's full attention, creating a type of emotional response that enhances one's memory, understanding, and usually implementation of the idea (Fogarty, 2002). Because teachers readily understand the importance of students' success, they stand ready to implement innovations guaranteed to boost their students' comprehension and achievement. When enough teachers implement any innovation, change can become contagious (Fullan, 2007; Kaagan, 2009). Since the key to creating better teaching is knowledge and implementation of research-based innovations and techniques, adequate professional training is an important first step.

Creating a rewarding adult learning experience isn't completely the job of the professional development educator. Assisting adults in learning requires a shared responsibility. In other words, the responsibility for learning rests on the shoulders of both the educator and the student, especially when that student is an adult (Taylor, Marienau, & Fiddler, 2000). And a lot can be done to motivate learning and growth.

Adults, again are most motivated when the topic or innovation is *useful* to them. This is why the PDLL in general recommend conducting a needs assessment, which enables them to collect data on what the prospective group of learners would find useful. Even so, sometimes the usefulness of an innovation isn't clear; so, it is important to communicate to one's audience precisely *how* the professional development sessions or programs will help them achieve their goals. Such information clarifies in teachers' minds how further professional development on their part will ultimately benefit their students. As noted earlier, one must constantly connect new learning to teachers' prior knowledge to enhance and maximize their retention and likely implementation of new ideas.

Even in an exceptional professional development session, some of those attending may lack motivation or not seem interested. At times there are obstacles to learning over which one has no control, such as a teacher's lack of confidence, a conflict in scheduling, or insufficient time to provide for the innovation's implementation. Whatever these obstacles, however, a well-planned and engaging session can usually overcome some of the obstructions. A few ways to overcome obstacles include collaborating with grade-level or content area teams, offering time to model and coach individual teachers on a one-on-one individual basis, and scheduling follow-up problem-solving sessions or related book discussions on the same subject.

Along with the PDLL, that advised us, we believe that a constructivist perspective is most useful in planning one's professional development sessions. Active participation, scaffolding, and co-constructed meaning based on dialogue and grounded in the school's culture are a means to adult learning. In professional development, this learning occurs best when opportunities are provided to increase the knowledge of the central actor– the teacher—through the combined knowledge of the school community. The beliefs, conceptual knowledge, and procedural knowledge readily accepted within the school community can be analyzed during professional development and as a result may be reconsidered or revised to good effect through such examination (Bruner, 1986; Fosnot, 1996; von Glasersfeld, 1996).

All those involved in professional development activities learn together. Slip-ups committed while implementing new ideas are embraced as harmless as group members dialogue about their experiences and concerns (von Glasersfeld, 1996). Wegner (2009) asserts that learning thereby becomes part of the school's identity, creating a "community of practice" (p. 212) where teachers are transformed in their thinking and practices.

With this perspective on the adult learning experience, next we explore how one should go about planning a professional development session for the first time. As noted by the PDLL, the first such session can be a nerve-racking ordeal, but with careful planning and organization the session will nonetheless be a success.

CONSIDERING A TOPIC FOR PROFESSIONAL DEVELOPMENT

Novice presenters should ideally plan to report only on topics about which they have expertise. It is easiest and most enjoyable to share with colleagues that which one knows best. Natural expertise enables a presenter to be ready to deal competently with any questions regarding practice, research, and resources. In addition, demonstrations, samples, and examples from experience lend credence and therefore enhance the learning experience for your audience (Bean, 2004).

With faculty and staff input, the District 13 Professional Development Committee was charged with the task of creating a professional development day—on a very small budget—with a focus on science. The science teacher, who was on the planning team, walked into Katherine's classroom one afternoon to ask if she would be a presenter. Katherine was completing her reading specialist coursework that spring, and although she was flattered to be asked to present, she declined. "I'm not an expert in science. There was simply no way I could do this!"

During the next day the superintendent visited Katherine while she was teaching. Such a visit was fairly common, so she thought nothing of it until he said, as he was walking out the door, "You are an excellent *reading* teacher. I want you to present at the District Science Day. Think about combining science and reading."

As Katherine reflected later, "I thought, 'Of course—integrating science and reading. I can do that,! And I *did*." Katherine realized that she needed to consider what she knew best and taught well in planning for her first formal presentation. That approach is what the PDLL would suggest as well. Think "I may not be able to present on _____, but I can present on _____." Katherine was not comfortable presenting materials just on science, but she could most certainly offer a session integrating science materials with reading instruction.

AN ASSESSMENT TO GUIDE PLANNING

The first step in planning a professional development session is to learn as much as possible about those who will be participating, because each person brings a variety of life experiences, skills, background knowledge, and learning styles (Bean, 2004). One way to learn about the participants and how to help with their reading concerns is to conduct a needs assessment.

A needs assessment provides information about the current practices of teachers and staff to determine what they want to learn or understand at a deeper level. Collecting the relevant information should be both easy and systematic, ideally. Simple formats include checklists or surveys that even the busiest of teachers can find time to complete and return. Information on specific needs can be gathered on site from observations, short informal conversations, or interviews. This quick survey is especially important because, as Guskey (2000) points out, "Although most educators can articulate the problems and difficulties they are experiencing, they may not be aware of their actual needs" (p. 57). Being able to identify needs readily and promptly is a good practice underlying the worthy aim of advancing exemplary reading methods and improving reading for all students.

Conducting needs assessments also confirms that the presenter is interested in what teachers know, but more importantly in what they want to learn. Renee conducted such an assessment before she met with the teachers for the first of a series of sessions. Teachers appreciate the bottom-up model, where they provide input for professional development goals and objectives. When teachers feel they are involved in the process of creating the agenda, they are usually motivated to actively participate, apply their new understanding, and carry on with positive changes that extend beyond the presentation and their individual classrooms. The change, of course, benefits students.

Creating the Needs Assessment

Gathering pertinent information to better inform professional development sessions for reading improvement is a wise and essential beginning. We recommended using surveys, checklists, and short, informal teacher interviews to facilitate creating a well-organized and well-conceived plan. Knowing that teachers are always short on time, the PDLLs who advised us believe a survey for all faculty and staff and a brief follow-up for clarity with just a sample of teachers and staff are appropriate.

Surveys can be specifically designed with the reading instruction culture of the school in mind. Figure 9.1 is an example of a survey created to gather information on literature circles by Connie, one of our PDLLs. The subject matter was very familiar to Connie, who as a beginner felt more comfortable presenting in an area of expertise.

After analyzing the needs assessment data, a sample of teachers attending the professional development sessions can be interviewed either in grade-level groups or individually to gather additional information or clarify data from the survey or checklist. In general, the survey follow-up should be very informal, resembling a discussion more than a question-and-answer session. Remember to acknowledge the teachers' wealth of knowledge while creating a professional development plan that builds on their prior knowledge *and* improves reading instruction. Sample questions in Table 9.1 are offered as a guide to developing even more questions to probe deeper into the reading needs of the faculty and staff.

Please take a few moments to complete this needs assessment and place it in my box by Monday, February 28th. Thank you!—*Connie*

1. Are you familiar with literature circles?   Yes   No

2. Have you received previous professional training on literature circles?   Yes   No

3. Are you implementing literature circles in your class?   Yes   No

4. If you answered "No" to #3, why not? _____

_____

5. What are you doing in your class to encourage students to read a variety of books? _____

_____

6. Which areas of literacy do you currently believe need more of your attention? Please rate them in order of importance, with 1 being the most important and 5 being the least important.

_____ phonics   _____ comprehension   _____ writing

_____ fluency   _____ vocabulary   _____ (other) _____

FIGURE 9.1. Sample needs assessment survey.

TABLE 9.1. Question Suggestions to Guide a Needs Assessment Interview

Learning about ...	Question suggestions
Teachers	• How do you feel about your reading instruction this year? • Talk about a lesson that went very well. • Talk about a lesson that you felt could have been much better. • What are some things that get in the way of good instruction?
School	• How does the school community support your reading instruction? • How does the principal support your reading instruction? • How can the school community, including the administrators, do a better job in supporting the reading achievement of students?
Student data	• Which reading assessments do you find particularly useful? • How do you analyze and use the reading assessment data? • What questions are not answered by the reading assessments you currently use?
Professional development assumptions	• You completed a survey asking for input on _____ for the upcoming professional development session. Please describe how you think this professional development topic will help with the reading achievement of students in the school. • What are your expectations for the professional development session? • What kinds of long-term support will help faculty members work together to achieve a level of success in this area of professional development?

Note. Adapted from Lyons and Pinnell (2001, p. 47).

Meeting with the school's principal or curriculum director to review the data is recommended, especially when presenting for the first time. Getting feedback from administrators can help with planning and boost confidence. Administrators have a unique understanding of the school community and curriculum as a whole that can benefit planning decisions.

Using the Needs Assessment Data to Plan

Dean (2004) suggests that decisions about the learning goals, objectives, and content of the professional development sessions should be based on a close analysis of the needs assessment data. Learning goals are specific statements about what one should know, do, or feel as a result of participation in professional development activities (p. 105). Learning objectives break down the goal into statements that explain exactly what is to be learned. The content, based on the goals and objectives, can include developing a more sophisticated understanding of a familiar reading topic, introducing innovative teaching processes, or exploring emerging research. These needs assessment data can help determine the kinds of reading instruction that are in need of support, which teaching strategies are already being used in classrooms, and any particular areas of interest that attendees might have. In addition, the needs assessment can shed light on how best to organize professional development activities (Guskey, 2000). With this information, an action plan can be designed for the professional development session.

To plan a series of professional development sessions on assessment, Mary Kay used a needs assessment that included both a checklist and open-ended questions, similar to the interest survey shown in Figure 9.1. The survey was sent to all of the district's principals, who in turn asked their schools' teachers to fill out the forms at their next faculty meeting. The completed surveys were then collected at the end of those same meetings and returned to Mary Kay via the postal service. This process look a bit longer than using Survey Monkey (*www.surveymonkey.com*), but the principals wanted to be sure that all the teachers were given sufficient time to thoughtfully complete the survey.

With the surveys back in hand, the checklist data were analyzed to determine which assessment topics were of greatest interest to most teachers who were planning to attend the sessions. To begin with, choices were generally divided into three categories: (1) topics with which teachers were familiar, (2) topics about which teachers wanted to learn, and (3) topics about which teachers were familiar but wanted more knowledge. Next a tally of total responses was calculated per topic based on the prepared checklist of topic choices. A sample of the data analysis is presented in Table 9.2. Among teachers who completed the needs assessment, 15 wanted to learn about matching standards to assessments and 12 wanted to learn about collecting and managing assessment data.

TABLE 9.2. Analysis of the Reading Assessment Needs Assessment Data

Topics with which teachers were familiar	No. of responses	Topics about which teachers wanted to learn	No. of responses	Topics in which teachers wanted more knowledge	No. of responses
Running records	53	Matching standards to assessments	15	Comprehension	52
Anecdotal records	50			Phonics	41
Checklists	50	Collecting and managing assessment data	12	Spelling inventories	38
Comprehension	42			Informal reading inventories	36
Beginning letter sounds	15	Spelling inventories	10		
		Time-efficient testing	5	Assessment batteries	30
Portfolios	11	Teacher-made tests	5	Portfolios	26
Informal assessments	3	Assessing nonreaders	2	Phonemic awareness	26
				Running records	15
		Report card grading	2		

The checklist data showed that the teachers had knowledge of, but wanted additional information in, the areas of comprehension, phonics, and spelling inventories.

Based on the data analyzed from the survey, Mary Kay decided to offer three sessions of professional development training: Session 1 would focus on phonics assessments and how to match standards with assessments, Session 2 on spelling inventories and informal reading inventories (IRI), and Session 3 on comprehension assessments and the collection and management of assessment data. Interestingly, comprehension was mentioned on 42 surveys as an assessment topic that was familiar; however, comprehension was also checked on 52 surveys as a topic about which teachers wanted to learn. To glean more information, Mary Kay asked the teachers about comprehension assessments in her conversations with teachers and staff. Specifically, she asked grade level teams to comment on which comprehension assessments were familiar and unfamiliar.

Because of the needs assessment survey and follow-up, sessions focused on the subject matter about which teachers most wanted to learn. The plan for all three professional development sessions was shared with teachers at the first of three meetings. Teachers were made aware of the agenda, the data to support the agenda, and the learning goals and objectives for each session. This sharing was important for a clear and mutual understanding of the tasks and expectations (Taylor et al., 2000).

Connie's Experience

Planning professional development curricula based on needs data is standard procedure, but occasionally a literacy leader may be approached to facilitate a particular professional development session because he or she is regarded as an expert in a particular area of literacy. Connie was considered the faculty's literature circle "expert" because her students were involved in literature circles over the course of several years. Thus, because of her relative expertise, Connie was asked to help with a professional development session on literature circles. She felt confident in planning and presenting—even though it was her first professional development experience—because of her knowledge in this area. Bean (2004) put it bluntly when she wrote "Know your stuff" (p. 98), and after years of reading widely and perfecting the management and implementation of literature circles Connie knew her stuff!

After agreeing to present, Connie wanted to develop a needs assessment to gather information about her colleagues' knowledge of literature circles to help design the presentation. She thought about her colleagues' varied experiences with literature circles and how she could support both those new to the technique and those who had had experience with them. She also wanted to highlight the many standards addressed when implementing literature circles along with how literature circles motivate students to read for pleasure. Connie developed the needs assessment survey cited earlier in Figure 9.1 to gather the data she required.

The first four questions helped Connie understand respondents' general familiarity with literature circles. The fifth question sought information on colleagues' literacy practices in general so that Connie could explicitly show how literature circles were connected to the reading standards. Specifically, this question sought to determine how her colleagues were encouraging students to be motivated to read so that Connie could highlight how literature circles encourage reading for pleasure. The final question allowed Connie to focus on instructional topics that teachers viewed as needing attention, so these topics might be integrated into the literature circle presentation or addressed at a later date. With the data Connie collected, she was able to design a presentation that matched the unique needs of her colleagues.

AN INVITING ENVIRONMENT

With the needs assessment completed, it is time to consider *where* the professional development session should be held. Adults learn best in a professional environment where they can feel at ease (Bean, 2009). The ideal setting for learning could be the school—but equally well it also could be the public library, the local hotel, or even a business conference center. Mary Kay remembers professional development sessions held at Allstate Insurance's corporate headquarters in Northbrook, Illinois. "It was so relaxing for all of us to spend the day away from our classrooms and offices. We were made to feel very important and welcomed. We used Allstate's auditorium, meeting rooms, and cafeteria. At the end of the day we felt refreshed and ready to try the innovations presented that day."

Even if no major corporation volunteers its facilities for your instructional sessions, your learning environment should still be inviting. It ought to have comfortable seating that can be arranged for small- and whole-group work where the facilitator can move around easily. Silberman (2005) suggests that tables and chairs should be arranged in the shape of a *U* or *V*, with the open end facing the front, as this arrangement allows for a variety of opportunities for participants to share and discuss.

The room temperature should be such that participants are not too cold or warm, and the lighting natural whenever possible. There should be little clutter and enough space for those attending to engage in the planned activities. The room must also be able to accommodate the technology needed for the presentation.

A PROFESSIONAL DEVELOPMENT DESIGN
WITH ENGAGEMENT IN MIND

As noted earlier, first time presenters especially should seriously consider sharing information only on subjects in which they have expertise. It is easier and fun to share what one knows best. Personal expertise enables a presenter to be ready for just about anything—including questions regarding practice, research, and resources. Demonstrations, samples, and examples from your own experience lend a presentation greater credence and clout with an adult audience (Bean, 2004). For example, Connie's presentation on literature circles was a success owing in part to her knowledge about and automatic comfort with the topic. She had the requisite experience, knew the relevant research, and was ready to model, coach, and be a resource for others.

Consider the length of the session when planning, and begin and end the session on time. If the session is scheduled to start at 4:00 P.M. and end at 6:00 P.M., be sure that's what happens. Develop some variety in the activities so that participants are able to sit, move around a bit, discuss, think, and plan. By allowing for some informality, participants stay engaged, active, and attentive.

Adults need some respite; so, be sure to offer a 10-minute break for every hour to hour and a half of presentation time to allow for conversation, a short stretch, and a visit to the restroom. Although a break of 10 minutes seems appropriate for groups of 20 or less, larger groups may need a break of 15 minutes, especially if there aren't many available restrooms close to the meeting room.

If the session is after a hard day of work or on a teacher development day, a refreshing snack is always welcomed. Provide fruit or veggies cut into bite-sized pieces set on tables with plates, napkins, and forks about 10 minutes before the session is scheduled to start. This welcomes guests and subtly suggests that they begin gathering in the prepared seating arrangement. After a break, when participants get their blood flowing again, a bite of chocolate seems to be the perfect trick to bring them back and provide the energy for more learning. Check well in advance with administrators to make sure that it is acceptable to serve treats and that there is a is budget to provide for them.

Although it is always considerate to start on time, a few participants may be late in arriving. To accommodate those who arrive late, begin the session with time for participants to engage in an introduction that builds a sense of community by learning about colleagues' interests beyond those in education. For example, Ayn's favorite opener is called "two fibs and one fact." In this activity, individuals list three events—one that actually occurred and two that did not. Once written down on pieces of paper, the events are shared in small groups, and those in the group have to decide which statement reveals the fact. Usually there are lots of smiles, laughter, and "I didn't know that," heard over and over. Relaxed and feeling connected, participants are then ready to listen and engage.

When considering the remainder of the session, all components should be tied together with threads that are made explicit to those in attendance. For example, the various activities in Connie's presentation were connected to the planning and implementation of literature circles. The strategies and activities should be useful and appealing so that teachers begin to use them right away. Strategy instruction should include implementation but also the research or theories that support it. Discuss when teachers can use a particular strategy and why students benefit from it. Model the strategy and then provide the guidance to allow teachers to engage in the implementation themselves. Plan activities that allow for active participation, small- and whole-group discussion, individual reflection, and the sharing of what is already known about a topic connected to new knowledge from the professional development session.

Another way to foster connectedness and engagement is to use the KWL (Ogle, 1986) strategy to (1) give participants a chance to chat, (2) encourage talk about what is already known (what we **k**now) about the topic, and (3) formulate questions related to the topic. In this way, one models the strategy but also immediately engages other adults in the strategy.

Gathering participant questions in a KWL (what we **w**ant to know) (Ogle, 1986) can not only help the presenter begin to connect with the participants but also validate the importance of their questions, comments, and stories of reading instruction successes and challenges. This technique helps establish trust, build rapport, and bring value to participants' voices and experiences. This sense of trust and rapport helps those attending the session to feel safe enough to share, ask questions without feeling embarrassed, and **l**earn.

Reflection

The goal of any professional development presentation is to share something new and meaningful with participants in the hope that they find it efficacious and therefore worth implementing. To ensure ample time to process new information and consider how best to implement what one has learned, it is important to provide activities for thoughtful reflection. Adults need ample time to process new information and connect it with the methods they are currently using (Sylwester, 1995). Reflective activities provide time to assimilate ideas and personalize learning both during and after the presentation (see Figure 9.2).

With appealing teaching ideas, teachers will want to begin using the strategies and activities with their students right away, and written reflection can provide the framework to nudge them to begin using the information immediately and over time. Reflection provides time for teachers to consider their current practices and describe in writing

---

Please take a minute to reflect on your learning by completing each sentence.

I was excited to learn . . .

I was surprised . . .

I was concerned . . .

I am still wondering . . .

FIGURE 9.2. Samples of reflection sentence starters.

how their new knowledge can be integrated into the school day (Hyde, 1992). Furthermore, collaborative time with grade-level or subject area colleagues enables one to build confidence that may be needed to try something new (Miller, 1992; Schmoker, 2006).

INVITATIONS

Once there is a clear understanding of teachers' needs and a plan for how those needs can be met with literacy strategies and activities, an invitation can be sent and posters placed in school buildings to advertise the professional development event. The PDLLs who advised us recommended sending invitations even when teachers are required to attend. The invitation lets those attending become more aware well in advance of specifically what will be covered in the training (see the sample invitation shown in Figure 9.3).

    Be sure to invite the principal, curriculum director, and reading specialist to attend the session as well. It is important to include administrators and reading and educational specialists in professional development so that they are aware of what is being shared and can provide the encouragement, materials, and personnel needed for implementing.

ORGANIZATION AND PRACTICE

Once the professional development topic is selected, literacy strategies and activities chosen, and the program planned, it is time to get organized. Being well organized is one way to ensure a smoothy inacted and trouble-free event. Practice everything and keep track of the time it takes while practicing to stay within the allotted timeframe.

Learn Ways to Help Students Become Better Readers

Where   Academy Charter School Library

When   February 28th with snacks and beverages at 2:45

Time   Promptly at 3:00–4:15

Strategies include:

Read, Cover, Remember, Retell
Alpha-boxes

All district teachers are welcome!

Please forward any questions to
extension 1234 or *msmith@academy.com*

FIGURE 9.3. Sample of a professional development invitation. The strategies named in the invitation are from Hoyt (1999).

There are a variety of ways to organize, but we suggest creating separate piles of paper categorized by topic, with the materials set in the order that they will be used. This approaches ensures that nothing is skipped or forgotten. Walk though each step of the presentation, practicing what will be said and using all components of the presentation. After practicing, packing the materials for travel in the order on the agenda allows for ease in set up, presentation, and cleanup.

CONNECTING WITH THE PARTICIPANTS

With practice, a level of comfort and skill in making the presentation is produced, thereby enabling the presenter to be open with, connected, and responsive to the participants. This sense of confidence creates the "buy-in" that is necessary, especially when presenting something new. Being comfortable allows one to enjoy the experience and help those in attendance to relate to the information (Bean, 2004).

Another way to connect with the participants is to move around. A speaker that circulates keeps everyone focused, curious, and interested. Moving around also provides the opportunity to pause, think, and reduce any stress that may be experienced. Mingling among the audience members allows them to feel as though they are part of the action.

Speaking above the noise of an overhead projector or from a PowerPoint presentation is fairly common in professional development. Be sure to always project your voice in the direction of the other participants so that they won't miss a word.

Flexibility is a necessity that can also affect the presenter's relationship with those in attendance. Prepare for a presentation until it is known by heart, but understand that things may not always run the way they were planned. Be ready to say "I don't know" when unable to answer a question, but offer to research the answer. Bring extra copies of handouts, the name of a contact in the technology department to provide assistance with any technical issues, an overhead bulb, and an extension cord along with your materials. Bring pencils, pens, markers, and paper for those who may need supplies, and carry contact information in case participants want to get in touch with you later.

EVALUATING PROFESSIONAL DEVELOPMENT

Members of the PDLL group gauged the success of their sessions by the relative engagement of their participants, but formal evaluation was more effective in providing authoritative feedback. Evaluations help ascertain how the session was received as well as collect data on participants' questions and areas of need.

Penelope developed the evaluation form shown in Figure 9.4 for her first professional development session on double-entry journals, which she passed out at the conclusion of her presentation. Penelope decided she wanted the teachers to provide honest

Evaluation of the Double-Entry Journal Presentation

Please let me know if you plan to use the double-entry journal and jigsaw strategies. Then provide some feedback on the presentation.—*Penelope*

Return this form to me by **September 27th** for a literary treat! Thank you.

I plan to use some of the strategies I learned today.	Yes	No
I plan to use the jigsaw technique in my class.	Yes	No
I plan to use the double-entry journal in my class.	Yes	No

What did you find to be the most helpful? _____

_____

How can I provide a more interactive, engaging workshop? _____

_____

How can I continue to support you? _____

_____

Please let me know if you would like me to visit your class or provide more information on the collaborative group and/or double-entry journal process. Include your name and the questions/concerns you would like me to address.

FIGURE 9.4. An evaluation to provide feedback.

and thoughtful feedback; so, she asked them to complete and return the evaluation later. She put a deadline date on the evaluation and gave a small reward (e.g., candy or pencil) to those who returned the evaluation to her on time. With the data Penelope was able to not only critique herself but also follow up with the teachers who wanted support and more information.

SUPPORT IN THE FORM OF GOODIE BAGS

Often teachers are more willing to try something new if they are given all the tools they need for implementation. Our PDLL advisors suggest offering goodie bags that include any of the materials teachers would need the very next day to begin using what they learned from the presentation. For example, Linda taught her staff how to use post-it notes to support comprehension across the middle school curriculum. She gathered and organized post-it notes of various sizes that were already available in the staff room. As a parting gift, participants received goodie bags that held the set of post-it notes with reminders on how to use them. Coupled with her demonstrations and handouts, the teachers then had everything needed to begin supporting comprehension the very next day. But, while providing goodie bags is an excellent way to support teachers, the job is not yet done.

CONTINUED SUPPORT AND POSITIVE CHANGE

The professional development session was a success, and teachers are buzzing about the strategies introduced. Bravo! But to help ensure long-term and schoolwide implementation, don't stop now. Keep the teachers and staff motivated to use the new practices by continually engaging in problem solving, competency building, and discussions (Lambert, 1998; Wegner, 2009). Adults, just like children, need to feel intrinsic motivation, and trying new practices is a form of active learning that also motivates (Lyons & Pinnell, 2001; Wegner, 2009; Wlodkowski, 2004). Because of this motivation, faculty and staff members can support one another, problem-solve together, and collectively reflect on their teaching experiences at the staff level, grade level, whole-school level, and in program meetings (Lyons & Pinnell, 2001; Ogle, 2007).

The professional development session may have provided the impetus for change, but even as teachers employ the new strategies, they will continue to need support. Time is needed for proper implementation and integration into the curriculum with continued assistance. This assistance impacts practices in the classroom and throughout the school. Schmoker (2006) suggests that teachers should work in teams to promote, sustain, and maintain the work they begin in implementing new literacy activities and strategies. He also believes follow-up sessions where teachers share their experiences with the new techniques but also their evolving needs are needed for ultimate success.

STUDY GROUPS

Fullan (2006) explains that the power of teachers working together in their schools serves not only to motivate them but also to be a cog in the system that ensures change. While the presenter provides the initial impetus for change in the professional development session, the subsequent momentum that is created impacts teacher growth, which in turn impacts student learning. Used as a follow-up to professional development, study groups provide socialization and emotional support to sustain implementation (Brandt, 1998; Sylwester, 1998). Study groups also allow teachers to be in control of their learning while the group members encourage, motivate, and energize one another. Furthermore the leadership or facilitation role in study groups can be shared among group members (Bean, 2004; Reeves, 2006; Wenger, 2009; Wlodkowski, 2004).

Announce that a study group is being formed to continue investigating the professional development topic soon after the session. Serve as moderator for the first session, where the group brainstorms (1) how members should pursue their area of study (book club format, discussion of selected journal articles, jigsaw on various aspects of the topic); (2) when, where, and how often the group will meet; (3) who will facilitate each session; and (4) ways to empower one another to work as a community of teachers to ensure student literacy growth.

Although the agenda of the study group meeting is determined by the group itself, the PDLL advisors suggest a framework that includes:

- Shared reading and discussions. This time period allows the group to learn together as each member brings unique understandings of the reading to the group, thus co-creating meaning within the context of the school setting.

- Sharing stories of implementation. This time period allows the individual to be reflective but also for the group to learn from others' experiences and challenges.

- Peer coaching. This time period allows the group to improve, with "many minds working together" (Fullan, 2007, p. 301) to ensure success. Since colleagues are usually unable to observe one another teaching in person, a digital recording of lessons can be shared to discuss a lesson's development and effectiveness along with constructive thoughts for improvement.

Although a consistent agenda is recommended for each meeting, the study group's format should be flexible.

Materials for study include books, journal articles, videos, and podcasts, to name a few. The group will want to determine guidelines for choosing materials, but it is a good idea to start with a list of available resources and materials. With this list, the group can vote on possibilities or the facilitator of a session can select the best choices. Study groups are a meaningful way to build shared knowledge and invest in learning that results in greater student success.

ADDITIONAL CONSIDERATIONS

This chapter began with a story about Renee who, through hard work and reflection, has become an expert in facilitating professional development. She offers this additional advice when providing professional development:

- Needs assessments are valuable and should not be overlooked.
- Think of depth, not breadth. Explain one or two concepts or lessons in detail. Don't overdo it.
- Consider that most teachers want to know *what* to teach, not necessarily *how* to teach.
- Share the agenda before the session whenever possible.

- Smile—especially during introductions.
- Set learning goals for the session.
- Expect comments about time spent on research and theory; so, use a format like this:
  - Explain the theory in a simplified manner, using key phrases.
  - Immediately connect the theory to practice.
  - Model the lesson that connects with the theory.
  - Share stories about the theory and lesson.
  - Let teachers practice.
  - Ask who wants to read more on the topic. At that point, many teachers do!
- Use an explicit structure in the session. One might be:
  - Share the agenda.
  - Explain what to expect.
  - Introduce the theory and content, using key phrases that audience members will remember.
  - Demonstrate the strategy so that participants can implement it with their students.
  - Include reflection on the new learning.
- Understand that within a group there will be those who are positive, those who are undecided, and those who are negative. Support all three by asking them to fill in the blank: *I think I'd like to try* _____. Then they should commit to trying it.
- Listen carefully and respond thoughtfully when teachers share their concerns.
- Expect a wide range of learners. Some will learn immediately, while others may need to see the lesson modeled five times before they begin to understand.
- Let teachers know they will be supported beyond the professional development session.
- Set up experiences where teachers can support one another within the school and network outside of the school.
- Follow up with those who asked for assistance within a week.
- If feedback was requested in the form of an evaluation, share what was learned in a future professional development session or faculty meeting.

IMPLEMENTING KEY IDEAS

The PDLL team acknowledges that the information in this chapter reflects the best possible situations. Needs assessment participation isn't always high, and literacy leaders do not always have the option of presenting a topic on which they have a lot of expertise (Guskey, 1994). Nonetheless, the guidance presented is based on research and experience. Key ideas include:

- Develop, implement, and analyze a needs assessment whenever possible to guide your planning.
- Select a comfortable setting for the session.
- Create an engaging session that includes (1) an opening activity, (2) interactive participation, (3) thoughtful reflection, and (4) formalized evaluation.
- Organize your presentation and materials scrupulously.
- Practice a lot.
- Recommend next-day implementation of the new methods/techniques.
- Provide ongoing support for long-term change.

CONCLUDING THOUGHTS

Those who become literacy specialists do so with students' welfare uppermost in mind. Whenever one facilitates professional development in literacy for teachers, staff, and administrators, many students end up benefiting as the new strategies are implemented. School communities also benefit when long-term support leads to long-term organizational change. So, having read this chapter, don't wait to be asked to facilitate a professional development session. Volunteer!

References

Alexander, P. A., & Fox, E. (2004). A historical perspective on reading research and practice. In R. B. Ruddell & N. J. Unrau (Eds.), *Theoretical models and processes of reading* (5th ed., pp. 33–68). Newark, DE: International Reading Association.

Allington, R. (2001). *What really matters for struggling readers*. New York: Longman.

Allington R. (2006). *What really matters for struggling readers: Designing research-based programs* (2nd ed.). Boston: Pearson Allyn & Bacon.

Allington, R. (2008). *What really matters in response to intervention*. Boston: Allyn & Bacon.

Alvermann, D. E., Phelps, S. F., & Gillis, V. R. (2010). Content area reading and literacy: Succeeding in today's diverse classrooms (6th ed.). Boston: Pearson Allyn & Bacon.

Alvermann, D. E. (2001, October). *Effective literacy instruction for adolescents*. Paper commissioned by the National Reading Conference, Oak Creek, WI.

Anderson, R. (2004). Role of the reader's schema in comprehension, learning, and memory. In R. B. Ruddell & N. J. Unrau (Eds.), *Theoretical models and processes of reading* (5th ed., pp. 594–606). Newark, DE: International Reading Association.

Antil, L. R., Jenkins, J. R., Wayne, S. K., & Vadasy, P. F. (1998). Cooperative learning: Prevalence, conceptualizations, and the relation between research and practice. *American Educational Research Journal, 35,* 419–454.

Askew, S., & Lodge, C. (2001). Gifts, ping pong and loops: Linking feedback and learning. In S. Askew (Ed.), *Feedback for learning* (pp. 1–17). London: Routledge.

Bandura, A. (Ed.). (1997). *Self-efficacy: The exercise of control*. New York: Freeman.

Barnes, A. C., & Harlacher, J. E. (2008). Clearing the confusion: Response-to-intervention as a set of principles. *Education and Treatment of Children, 31*(3), 417–431.

Barr, R., Blachowicz, C. L. Z., & Buhle, R. (2004). *Illinois Snapshots of Early Literacy—K/1* (1st ed.). Springfield, IL: Illinois State Board of Education. Retrieved January 1, 2004, from *www.isbe.net/curriculum/reading/html/isel.*

Barth, B. M. (2000). The teachers' construction of knowledge. In J. Butcher, B. Moon, & E. Bird (Eds.). *Leading professional development in education* (pp. 187–199). London: Routledge.

Barth, R. (2002). The culture builder. *Educational Leadership, 59*(8), 6–11.

Bean, R. (2004). *The reading specialist: Leadership for the classroom, school, and community*. New York: Guilford Press.

Bean, R. (2009). *The reading specialist: Leadership for the classroom, school, and community*. (2nd ed.). New York: Guilford Press.

Bear, D., Invernizzi, M., Templeton, S., & Johnston, F. (2007). *Words their way*. New York: Pearson.

Berrill, D., Doucette, L., & Verhulst, D. (2006). *Tutoring adolescent readers*. Markham, Ontario: Pembroke.

Blachowicz, C. L. Z., & Fisher, P. J. (2001). *Teaching vocabulary in all classrooms*. Upper Saddle River, NJ: Prentice Hall.

Blachowicz, C. L. Z., Moskal, M. K., Massarelli, J. R., Obrochta, C. M., Fogelberg, E., & Fisher, P. (2006). "Everybody reads": Fluency as a focus for staff development. In T. Rasinski, C. Blachowicz, & K. Lems (Eds.), *Fluency instruction: Research-based best practices* (pp. 141–154). New York: Guilford Press.

Blum, T., Lipsett, L., & Yocum, D. (2002). Literature circles: A tool for self-determination in one middle school inclusive classroom. *Remedial and Special Education, 23*(2), 99–109.

Bocala, C., Mello, D., Reedy, K., & Lacireno-Paquet, N. (2009). *Features of state response to intervention initiatives in northeast and island region states* (Issues & Answers Report No. REL2009-083). Washington, DC: U.S. Department of Education Sciences, Institute of Education. Retrieved November 26, 2010, from *ies.ed.gov/ncee/edlabs/regions/northeast/pdf/ REL_2009083.pdf*.

Brandt, R. (1998). On using knowledge about our brain: A conversation with Robert Sylwester. In R. Sylwester (Ed.), *Student brains, schooling issues: A collection of articles* (pp. 3–8). Arlington Heights, IL: Skylight Professional Development.

Brownell, M. T. (2000). An interview with Dr. Michael Pressley. *Intervention in School and Clinic, 36,* 105–107.

Brozo, W. G. (2002). *To be a boy, to be a reader: Engaging teen and preteen boys in active literacy*. Newark, DE: International Reading Association.

Bruner, J. (1986). *Actual minds, possible worlds*. Cambridge, MA: Harvard University Press.

Buck, A. (2010). *The attitudes of adolescents' participation in silent sustained reading*. Unpublished master's thesis, Saint Mary's College of California, Moraga.

Burden, P. R., & Byrd, D. M. (1994). *Methods for effective teaching*. Boston: Allyn & Bacon.

Burns, B. (1999). *How to teach balanced reading and writing*. Arlington Heights, IL: Skylight Professional Development.

Bursuck, W. D., & Damer, M. (2007). *Reading instruction: For students who are at risk or have disabilities*. Boston: Pearson Allyn & Bacon.

California Commission on Teacher Credentialing. (2006, January 29). Teacher training program by school district. Retrieved October 7, 2009, from *info.ctc.ca.gov/fmi/xsl/pgm_by_dist/ default.html*.

Carney, J. M. (1999). How classrooms as cultures influence entire schools. *Primary Voices, K–6, 7*(3), 53.

Clay, M. M. (1987). Learning to be learning disabled. *New Zealand Journal of Educational Studies, 22,* 155–173.

Clay, M. M. (1991). *Becoming literate: The construction of inner control*. Portsmouth, NH: Heinemann.

Clay, M. M. (2006). *An observation survey of early literacy achievement.* Portsmouth, NH: Heinemann.

Codell, E. R. (2004). *How to get your child to love reading.* New York: Algonquin Books of Chapel Hill.

Coiro, J. (2003). Reading comprehension on the Internet. Expanding our understanding of reading comprehension to expand new literacies. *The Reading Teacher, 56,* 458–464.

Collins, S. (2008). *The hunger games.* New York: Scholastic. Retrieved November 27, 2010, from *www.suzannecollinsbooks.com.*

Collins, S. (2009). *Catching fire.* New York: Scholastic.

Collins, S. (2010). *Mockingjay.* New York: Scholastic.

Covey, S. (1989). *The seven habits of highly effective people.* New York: Free Press.

Cradler, J. (1996). *Implementing technology in education: Recent findings from research and evaluation studies.* Retrieved September 18, 2010, from *www.wested.org/techpolicy/recapproach. html.*

Crowley, J. (2006). *Mrs. Wishy Washy's farm.* New York: Penguin.

Cunningham, P. M., & Cunningham, J. W. (1992). Making words: Enhancing the invented spelling–decoding connection. *The Reading Teacher, 46,* 106–115.

Curtis, P. C. (1999). *Bud, not Buddy.* New York: Delacorte Books for Young Readers.

Dahl, R. (1961). *James and the giant peach.* New York: Puffin Books.

Dahl, R. (1964). *Charlie and the chocolate factory.* New York: Penguin.

Daniels, H. (2002). *Literature circles: Voice and choice in book clubs and reading groups* (2nd ed.). Markham, Ontario: Pembroke.

Daniels, H., & Zemelman, S. (2004). *Subjects matter: Every teacher's guide to content area reading.* Portsmouth, NH: Heinemann.

Darling-Hammond, L. (2009). Thoughts on teacher preparation. *Edutopia.* Retrieved February 21, 2011, from *www.edutopia.org/linda-darling-hammond-teacher-preparation.*

Davey, B. (1983). Think-aloud: Modeling the cognitive processes of reading comprehension. *Journal of Reading, 27*(1), 44–47.

Dean, G. (2004). Designing instruction. In M. W. Galbraith (Ed.), *Adult learning methods: A guide for effective instruction* (3rd ed., pp. 93–118). Malabar, FL: Krieger.

Deshler, D. D., Palinscar, A. S., Biancarosa, G., & Nair, M. (2007). *Informed choices for struggling adolescent readers: A research-based guide to instructional programs and practices.* Newark, DE: International Reading Association.

Deshler, R. T., Deshler, D. D., & Biancarosa, G. (2007). School and district change to improve adolescent literacy. In D. D. Deshler, A. S. Palinscar, G. Biancarosa, & M. Nair (Eds.), *Informed choices for struggling adolescent readers: A research-based guide to instructional programs and practices* (pp. 92–110). Newark, DE: International Reading Association.

Deutsch, M. (1962). Cooperation and trust: Some theoretical notes. In M. R. Jones (Ed.), *Nebraska symposium on motivation* (pp. 275–319). Lincoln: University of Nebraska Press.

Diablo Vista Middle School. (2010–2011). *School vision and mission statements.* Retrieved August 12, 2010, from *www.dvms.srvusd.k12.ca.us/vision.*

Dorn, L., French, C., & Jones, T. (1998). *Apprenticeship in literacy: Transitions across reading and writing.* York, ME: Stenhouse.

Dowswell, P. (2003). *True stories of the second world war.* New York: Scholastic.

Dyer, H. (2004). *The fish in room 11.* New York: Scholastic.

Education Week. (2004, September 21). *Professional development*. Retrieved August 11, 2010, from *www.edweek.org/ew/issues/professional-development*.

Eisner, E. (2002). The kinds of schools we need. *Phi Delta Kappan, 83*(8), 578–583.

Elish-Piper, L. (2008). Overcoming common myths about parent involvement. *Illinois Reading Council Journal, 37*(1), 51–54.

Fisher, D., & Frey, N. (2004). *Improving adolescent literacy: Strategies at work*. Upper Saddle River, NJ: Pearson Merrill Prentice Hall.

Fletcher, R. (2006). *Boy writers: Reclaiming their voices*. Portland, ME: Stenhouse.

Fogarty, R. (2002). *Brain-compatible classrooms* (2nd ed.). Arlington Heights, IL: Skylight Professional Development.

Fogarty, R., & Pete, B. (2007). *From staff room to classroom: A guide to planning and coaching professional development*. Thousand Oaks, CA: Corwin Press.

Fosnot, C. T. (1996). Constructivism: A psychological theory of learning. In C. T. Fosnot (Ed.), *Constructivism: Theory, perspectives, and practice* (pp. 8–33). New York: Teachers College Press.

Fountas, I., & Pinnell, G. S. (2000). *Guiding readers and writers*. Portsmouth, NH: Heinemann.

Frazee, B., & Rudnitski, R. A. (1995). *Integrated teaching methods*. Albany, NY: Delmar.

Freeman, Y. S., & Freeman, D. E. (2009). *Academic language for English language learners and struggling readers: How to help students succeed across content areas*. Portsmouth, NH: Heinemann.

Fuchs, D., Compton, D. L, Fuchs, L. S., & Bryant, J. (2008). Making "secondary intervention" work in a three-tier responsiveness-to-intervention model: Findings from the first-grade longitudinal reading study at the National Research Center on Learning Disabilities. *Reading and Writing: An Interdisciplinary Journal, 21,* 413–436.

Fuchs, D., & Fuchs, L. S. (1998). Preparing special-needs students for reintegration: Curriculum-based measurement's impact on transenvironmental programming. *Journal of Learning Disabilities, 31,* 615–624.

Fuchs, L. S., Fuchs, D., & Zumeta, R. O. (2008). A curricular sampling approach to progress monitoring: Mathematics concepts and applications. *Assessment for Effective Intervention, 33,* 225–233.

Fullan, M. (2006). *Turnaround leadership*. San Francisco: Jossey-Bass.

Fullan, M. (2007). *The new meaning of educational change* (4th ed.). New York: Teachers College Press.

Gaskins, I. W. (2005). *Success with struggling readers: The Benchmark School approach*. New York: Guilford Press.

Gauthier, M., de Lisle, P., Holmgren, A., Mair, N., Sclar, M., Sheppard, D., et al. (2006–2007). *Boys and digital literacy: Summary report*. International Boys' Schools Coalition (IBSC). Retrieved July 10, 2010, from *www.theibsc.org/uploaded/IBSC/Action_Reseach/Boys_and_Digital_Literacy_Summary_Report_2007.pdf*.

George, K. O. (2002). *Swimming upstream: Middle school poems*. New York: Clarion Books.

Gérard, F., & Widener, J. (1999). A SMARTer way to teach foreign language: The SMART board interactive whiteboard as a language learning tool. Retrieved November 26, 2010, from *downloads01.smarttech.com/media/research/international_research/usa/sbforeignlanguage-class.pdf*.

Gillespie, P., & Lerner, N. (2008). *The Longman guide to peer tutoring.* New York: Pearson.

Glover, D., Miller D., Averis, D. & Door V. (2005). Leadership implications of using interactive whiteboards: Linking technology and pedagogy in the management of change. *Management in Education, 18*(5), 27–30.

Goldberg, G. L., & Rosswell, B. S. (2002). *Reading, writing, and gender: Instructional strategies and classroom activities that work for girls and boys.* Larchmont, NY: Eye on Education.

Goldenberg, C. (2008). Teaching English language learners: What the research does—and does not—say. *American Educator, 32*(2), 8–44. Retrieved October 5, 2009, from *www.aft.org/pubs-reports/american_educator/issues/summer08/goldenberg.pdf.*

Gordon, E. E. (2005). *Peer tutoring: A teacher's resource guide.* Lanham, MD: Scarecrow Education.

Gunning, T. G. (2008). *Developing higher-level literacy in all students: Building reading, reasoning, and responding.* Boston: Pearson Allyn & Bacon.

Guskey, T. R. (1994, April). *Professional development in education: In search of the optimal mix.* Paper presented at the annual meeting of the American Educational Research Association, New Orleans. Retrieved November 7, 2010, from *eric.ed.gov/PDFS/ED369181.pdf.*

Guskey, T. R. (2000). *Evaluating professional development.* Thousand Oaks, CA: Corwin Press.

Guzzetti, B. J., Young, P. J., Gritsavage, M. M., Fyfe, L. M., & Hardenbrook, M. (2002). *Reading, writing, and gender in literacy learning.* Newark, DE: International Reading Association.

Habrouch, J. E., Woldbeck, T., Ihnot, C., & Parker, R. I. (1999). One teacher's use of curriculum-based measurement: A changed opinion. *Learning Disabilities Research and Practice, 14*(2), 118–126.

Hagood, M. C., Stevens, L. P., & Reinking, D. (2003). What do THEY have to teach US?: Talkin' 'cross generations! In D. Alvermann (Ed.), *Adolescents and literacies in a digital world* (pp. 68–83). New York: Lang.

Harris, T. L., & Hodges, R. E. (Eds.). (1995). *The literacy dictionary: The vocabulary of reading and writing.* Newark, DE: International Reading Association.

Harste, J. C., Woodward, V. A., & Burke, C. L. (1986). *Language stories and literacy lessons.* Portsmouth, NH: Heinemann.

Hersch, P. (1998–1999). *A tribe apart: A journey into the heart of the American teenager.* New York: Random House.

Horowitz, A. (2000). *Stormbreaker.* New York: Penguin. Retrieved November 27, 2010, from *www.anthonyhorowitz.com.*

Hoyt, L. (1999). Revisit, reflect, retell. Portsmouth, NH: Heinemann.

Huey, E. B. (1968) The psychology and pedagogy of reading. Cambridge, MA: MIT Press. (Original work published 1908)

Humphrey, K. L. (1996). *Pompeii: Nightmare at midday.* New York: Franklin Watts.

Hyde, A. A. (1992). Developing a willingness to change. In W. T. Pink & A. A. Hyde (Eds.), *Effective staff development for school change* (pp. 169–188). Norwood, NJ: Ablex.

Hyde, A. A., & Pink, W. T. (1992). Thinking about effective staff development. In W. T. Pink & A. Hyde (Eds.), *Effective staff development for school change* (pp. 3–29). Norwood, NJ: Ablex.

International Reading Association Board. (1999). *Using multiple methods of beginning reading instruction: A position statement.* Newark: DE. Retrieved August 11, 2010, from *www.reading.org/General/AboutIRA/PositionStatements/MultipleMethodsPosition.aspx.*

International Reading Association Board. (2000). *Excellent reading teachers: A position statement.* Newark: DE. Retrieved September 8, 2009, from *www.reading.org/General/AboutIRA/PositionStatements/ExcellentTeachersPosition.aspx.*

Jansen, B. J., Spink, A., & Saracevic, T. (2000). Real life, real users, and real needs: A study and analysis of user queries on the web. *Information Processing and Management, 36,* 207–227.

Johns, J. L. (2008). *Basic reading inventory: Preprimer through grade twelve and early literacy assessments.* Dubuque, IA: Kendall Hunt.

Johnson, D. W., Johnson, R. T., & Holubec, E. J. (1993). *Circles of learning: Cooperation in the classroom* (4th ed.). Edina, MN: Interaction.

Johnston, P. H., & Nichols, J. (1995). Voices we want to hear and voices we don't. *Theory Into Practice, 34*(2), 94–100.

Joyce, B., & Showers, B. (2002). *Student achievement through staff development.* Alexandria, VA: Association for Supervision and Curriculum Development.

Justice, L. M., Invernizzi, M. A., & Meier, J. D. (2002). Designing and implementing an early literacy screening protocol: Suggestions for the speech–language pathologist. *Language, Speech, and Hearing Services in Schools, 33,* 84–101.

Kaagan, S. S. (2009). 30 reflective staff development exercises for educators (2nd ed.). Thousand Oaks, CA: Corwin Press.

Katz, C., & Kirby, S. (2001–2002). Literature circles. *Book Links, 11*(3), 41–43.

Kaiser Family Foundation. (2010, January). *Generation M2: Media in the lives of 8–18 year olds.* Kaiser Family Foundation Study. Retrieved November 26, 2010, from *www.kff.org/entmedia/mh012010pkg.cfm.*

Kinzer, C. K., & Leander, K. (2003). Technology and the language arts: Implications of an expanded definition of literacy. In J. Flood, D. Lapp, J. R. Squire, & J. M. Jensen (Eds.), *Handbook of research on teaching the English language arts* (2nd ed., pp. 546–566). Mahwah, NJ: Erlbaum.

Klein, M. L., Peterson, S., & Simington, L. (1991). *Teaching reading in the elementary grades.* Boston: Allyn & Bacon.

Kline, S. (1990). *Horrible Harry's secret* New York: Puffin Books. Retrieved November 27, 2010, from *www.suzykline.com/Book_List.html.*

Knowles, E., & Smith, M. (2005). *Boys and literacy: Practical strategies for librarians, teachers, and parents.* Westport, CT: Libraries Unlimited.

Kong, A., & Fitch, E. (2002–2003). Using book clubs to engage culturally and linguistically diverse learners in reading, writing and talking about books. *The Reading Teacher, 56*(4), 352–362.

Lambert, L. (1998). *Building leadership capacity in schools.* Alexandria, VA: Association for Supervision and Curriculum Development.

Langer, J. (1992). Rethinking literature instruction. In J. Langer (Ed.), *Literature instruction: A focus on student response* (pp. 35–53). Urbana, IL: National Council of Teachers of English.

Langer, J. A. (1995). *Envisioning literature: Literacy understanding and literature instruction.* New York: Teachers College Press.

Langer, J. A., & Flihan, S. (2000). Writing and reading relationships: Constructive tasks. In R. Indrisano & J. Squire (Eds.), *Perspectives on writing: Research, theory, and practice* (pp. 112–139). Newark, DE: International Reading Association.

Lankshear, C., & Knobel, M. (2003). *New literacies: Changing knowledge in the classroom.* Buckingham, UK: Open University Press.

LePell, M. C. (2002). *Hewlett final report.* Archives of Schools' Partnership for Institutional Reform through Adolescent Literacy (SPIRAL), Saint Mary's College of California, Moraga.

LePell, M. C. (2003). *Hewlett final report.* Archives of Schools' Partnership for Institutional Reform through Adolescent Literacy (SPIRAL), Saint Mary's College of California, Moraga.

LePell, M. C. (2004). *Professional development outline.* Archives of Schools' Partnership for Institutional Reform through Adolescent Literacy (SPIRAL), Saint Mary's College of California, Moraga.

Leslie, L., & Caldwell, J. S. (2010). *Qualitative Reading Inventory* (5th ed.). Boston: Allyn & Bacon.

Leu, D. J., Jr., & Kinzer, C. K. (2000). The convergence of literacy instruction and networked technologies for information and communication. *Reading Research Quarterly, 35,* 108–127.

Leu, D. J., Kinzer, C., Coiro, J., & Cammack, D. (2004). Toward a theory of new literacies emerging from the Internet and other information and communication technologies. *Reading Online.* Retrieved February 21, 2011, from *www.readingonline.org/newliteracies/lit_index.asp?HREF=/newliteracies/leu..*

Lewis, C., & Finders, M. (2002). Implied adolescent and implied teachers: A generation gap for new times. In D. E. Alvermann (Ed.), *Adolescents and literacies in a digital world* (pp. 101–113). New York: Peter Lang.

Long, H. B. (2004). Understanding adult learners. In M. W. Galbraith (Ed.), *Adult learning methods: A guide for effective instruction* (3rd ed., pp. 23–37). Malabar, FL: Krieger.

Lyons, C. A. (2003). Teaching struggling readers: How to use brain-based research to maximize learning. Portsmouth, NH: Heinemann.

Lyons, C. A., & Pinnell, G. S. (2001). *Systems for change in literacy education: A guide to Professional development.* Portsmouth, NH: Heinemann.

Manzo, A. (1969). The ReQuest procedure. *Journal of Reading, 13,* 123–127.

McCormick, L. (2010). *Parent involvement and student achievement.* Unpublished master's thesis, Saint Mary's College of California, Moraga.

McCray, A. D., Vaughn, S., & Neal, L. I. (2001), Not all students learn to read by third grade: Middle school students speak out about their reading disabilities. *Journal of Special Education, 35*(1), 17–30.

McKenna, M. C., & Kear, D. J. (1990). Measuring attitude toward reading: A new tool for teachers. *The Reading Teacher, 43,* 626–639.

Miller D., & Glover, D. (2002). The interactive whiteboard as a force for pedagogic change: The experience of five elementary schools in an English education authority. *Information Technology in Childhood Education Annual.* Available at *www.aace.org/DLindex.cfm/fuseaction/view/paperid/9117.*

Miller, L. (1992). Curriculum work as staff development. In W. T. Pink & A. A. Hyde (Eds.), *Effective staff development for school change* (pp. 93–108). Norwood, NJ: Ablex.

Miners, Z., & Pascopella, A. (2007, October). The new literacies. *District Administrator, 43*(10), 26–34.

Morris, D. (2002). *The Howard Street tutoring manual: Teaching at-risk readers in the primary grades.* New York: Guilford Press.

Morris, D. (2005). *The Howard Street tutoring manual: Teaching at-risk readers in the primary grades* (2nd ed.). New York: Guilford Press.

Morrow, L. M. (2009). *Literacy development in the early years: Helping children read and write.* Boston: Pearson Allyn & Bacon.

Moskal, M. K., & Blachowicz, C. (2006). *Partnering for fluency.* New York: Guilford Press.

Muth, K. D., & Alvermann, D. E. (1992). *Teaching and learning in the middle grades.* Boston: Allyn & Bacon.

"My Castro Valley History." (2009). *My Castro Valley: Your hometown website.* Retrieved November 28, 2010, from *www.mycastrovalley.com/history/page25.html.*

National Assessment of Educational Progress. (2010). *Reading: Grade 8 national results.* Retrieved February 17, 2011, from *nationsreportcard.gov/reading_2009/nat_g8.asp?subtab_ id=Tab_2&tab_id=tabl+tabsContainer.*

National Council of Teachers of English, Commission on Reading. (2004). *On reading, learning to read, and effective reading instruction: An overview of what we know and how we know it.* Retrieved September 30, 2009, from *www.ncte.org/positions/statements/onreading.*

National Endowment for the Arts. (1997). Survey of public participation. *Reading on the rise: A new chapter in American literacy.* Retrieved November 28, 2010, from *www.nea.gov/research/ ReadingonRise.pdf.*

National Endowment for the Arts. (2004). *Reading at risk: A survey of literacy reading in America. Executive summary* (Research Division Report No. 46). Retrieved August 23, 2010, from *www.arts.endow.gov/pub/RaRExec.pdf.*

National Endowment for the Arts. (2007). *To read or not to read: A question of national consequence* (Research Division Report No. 47). Retrieved February 19, 2011, from *www.nea.gov/ research/toread.pdf.*

National Endowment for the Arts. (2009). *Reading on the rise: A new chapter in American literacy.* Retrieved February 18, 2011, from *www.nea.gov/research/ReadingonRise.pdf.*

National Reading Panel. (2000). *Teaching children to read: Reports of the subgroups* (NIH Pub. No. 00–4754). Retrieved August 12, 2010, from *www.nationalreadingpanel.org/publications/ publications.htm.*

Neu, T. V., & Weinfeld, R. (2007). *Helping boys succeed in school.* Waco, TX: Prufrock Press.

Nevin, A., Thousand J., & Villa, R. (Eds.). (1994). *Creativity and collaborative learning: A practical guide to empowering students and teachers.* Baltimore: Brookes.

Newkirk, T. (2002). *Misreading masculinity: Boys literacy, and popular culture.* Portsmouth, NH: Heinemann.

North Central Regional Educational Library. (1996). *The definition of reading.* Retrieved September 8, 2009, from *www.ncrel.org/sdrs/areas/issues/content/cntareas/reading/li7lk1. htm.*

Nunan, D., & Lamb, C. (1996). *The self-directed teacher: Managing the learning process.* Cambridge, UK: Cambridge University Press.

O'Brien, D. (2001). "At-risk" adolescents: Redefining competence through the multiliteracies of intermediality, visual arts, and representation. *Reading Online, 4*(11). Retrieved December 15, 2009, from *www.readingonline.org/newliteracies/lit_index.asp?HREF=/newliteracies/ obrien/index.html.*

Ogle, D. (1986). K–W–L: A teaching model that develops active reading of expository text. *The Reading Teacher, 39,* 564–571.

Ogle, D. (2007). *Coming together as readers: Building literacy teams* (2nd ed.). Thousand Oaks, CA: Corwin Press.

Orlich, D. C., Harder, R. J., Callahan, R. C., Kauchak, D. P., & Gibson, H. W. (1994). *Teaching strategies: A guide to better instruction* (4th ed.). Lexington, MA: Heath.

Ornstein, A. C. (1995). *Strategies for effective teaching* (2nd ed.). Madison, WI: Brown & Benchmark.

Padak, N., & Rasinski, T. (2007). Is being wild about Harry enough?: Encouraging independent reading at home. *The Reading Teacher, 61,* 350–353.

Palmer, P. (2007). *The courage to teach*. San Francisco: Jossey-Bass.

Paris, S. G., Wasik, B. A., & Turner, J. C. (1991). The development of strategic readers. In R. Barr, M. L. Kamil, P. B. Rosenthal, & P. D. Pearson (Eds.), *Handbook of reading research* (Vol. II, pp. 609–640). New York: Longman.

Pearson PsychCorp. (2010). AIMSweb. Retrieved November 26, 2010, from *www.aimsweb.com*.

Peterson, R. (1992). *Life in a crowded place: Making a learning community*. Portsmouth: NH: Heinemann.

Pilgreen, L. J. (2000). *The SSR handbook: How to organize and maintain a silent sustained reading program*. Portsmouth, NH: Heinemann Boynton/Cook.

Pink, W. T., & Hyde, A. A. (1992). Doing effective staff development. In W. T. Pink & A. A. Hyde (Eds.), *Effective staff development for school change* (pp. 259–292). Norwood, NJ: Ablex.

Pressley, M. (2002). *Reading instruction that works: The case for balanced teaching* (2nd ed.). New York: Guilford Press.

Radtke, J. M. (1998). *How to write a mission statement*. The Grantsmanship Center. Retrieved September 10, 2009, from *www.tgci.com/magazine/How%20to%20Write%20a%20Mission%20Statement.pdf*.

Rae, T., & Pederson, L. (2007). *Developing emotional literacy with teenage boys: Building confidence, self-esteem, and self-awareness*. London: Chapman.

Raphael, T. (1986). Teaching question answer relationships, revisited. *The Reading Teacher, 39,* 516–522.

Raphael, T., Goatley, V., McMahon, S., & Woodman, D. (1995). Promoting meaningful conversations in student book clubs. In N. Roser & M. Martinez (Eds.), *Book talk and beyond: Children and teachers respond to literature* (pp. 66–79). Newark, DE: International Reading Association.

Raphael, T., Kehus, M., & Damphousse, K. (2001). *Book club for middle school*. Lawrence, MA: Small Planet Communications.

Raphael, T. E., & McMahon, S. I. (1997). Preface. In S. I. McMahon, T. E. Raphael, V. J. Goatley, & L. S. Pardo (Eds.), *The book club connection: Literacy learning and classroom talk* (pp. ix–xv). New York: Teachers College Press.

Rasinski, T. V., & Padak, N. (2009). Write soon. *The Reading Teacher, 62,* 618–620.

Rasinski, T. V. (2004). Creating fluent readers. *Educational Leadership, 61*(6), 46–51.

Reed, J. B, & Meyer, R. J. (2007). Edmund Burke Huey (1870–1913): A brief life with an enduring legacy. In S. E. Israel & E. J. Monaghan (Eds.), *Shaping the reading field: The impact of early reading pioneers, scientific research, and progressive ideas* (pp. 159–175). Newark, DE: International Reading Association. Retrieved September 12, 2009, from *www.reading.org/Publish.aspx?page=bk598-7Israel.pdf&mode=retrieve&D=10.1598/0872075986.&Fbk598-7-Israel.pdf&key=39500E32-D71B-4549-B6C0-E241689193D2*.

Reeves, D. B. (2006). *The learning leader: How to focus school improvements for better results*. Alexandria, VA: Association for Supervision and Curriculum Development.

Risko, V. J., & Walker-Dalhouse, D. (2009). Parents and teachers: Talking with or past one another—or not talking at all. *The Reading Teacher, 62,* 442–444.

Rogoff, B. (1990). *Apprenticeship in thinking: Cognitive development in social context.* New York: Oxford University Press.

Roller, G., & Fielding, L. (1998). Reflections. *Primary Voices, K–6, 7*(1), 37–43.

Rosenblatt, L. M. (2004). The transactional theory of reading and writing. In R. B. Ruddell & Unrau, N. J. (Eds.), Theoretical models and processes of reading (5th ed., pp. 1363–1398). Newark, DE: International Reading Association.

Saphier, J., & King, M. (1985). Good seeds grow in strong cultures. *Educational Leadership, 42*(6), 67–74.

Schirmer, B. R. (2010). *Teaching the struggling reader.* Boston: Pearson Allyn & Bacon.

Schlagel, R. (1982). *A qualitative inventory of word knowledge: A developmental study of Spelling, grades one through six.* Unpublished doctoral dissertation, University of Virginia, Charlottesville.

Schneider, M. T. (1992). Shared leadership in staff development. In W. T. Pink & A. A. Hyde (Eds.), *Effective staff development for school change* (pp. 237–256). Norwood, NJ: Ablex.

Schmidt, D. V., Sharp, R., & Stephens, T. (2001). No more "making nice." In H. T. Sockett, E. K. DeMulder, P. LePage, & D. R. Woods (Eds.), *Transforming teacher education: Lessons in professional development* (pp. 145–153). Westport, CT: Bergin & Garvey.

Schmoker, M. (2006). *Results now: How we can achieve unprecedented improvements in teaching and learning.* Alexandria, VA: Association for Supervision and Curriculum Development.

Schunk, D. H., & Zimmerman, B. J. (1997). Developing self-efficacious readers and writers: The role of social and self-regulatory processes. In J. T. Guthrie & A. Wigfield (Eds.), *Reading engagement: Motivating readers through integrated instruction* (pp. 34–50). Newark, DE: International Reading Association.

Scieszka, J. (2005). *Guys write for guys read.* New York: Viking.

Selden, G. (1960). *Cricket in Times Square.* New York: Bantam Doubleday.

Sellars, L. (1998). Helping one another across the generations. *Phi Delta Kappan, 79,* 94–98.

Sergiovanni, T. (1994). *Building community in schools.* San Francisco: Jossey-Bass.

Shepard, L. A. (2004). The role of assessment in a learning culture. In R. B. Ruddell & N. A. Unrau (Eds.), Theoretical models and processes of reading (5th ed., pp. 1614–1635). Newark, DE: International Reading Association.

Silberman, M. (2005). *101 ways to make training active* (2nd ed.). San Francisco: Pfeiffer.

Smith, M. W., & Wilhelm, J. D. (2006). *Going with the flow: How to engage boys (and girls) in their literacy learning.* Portsmouth, NH: Heinemann.

Smolin, L. I., & Lawless, K. A. (2003). Becoming literate in the technological age: New responsibilities and tools for teachers. *The Reading Teacher, 56,* 570–577.

Snow, C. E., Burns, M. S., & Griffin, P. (1998). *Preventing reading difficulties in young children.* Washington, DC: National Academy Press.

Snyder, Z. K. (1967). *The Egypt game.* New York: Atheneum.

Solvie, P. A. (2001). *The digital whiteboards as a tool in increasing student attention during early literacy instruction.* Retrieved November 26, 2010, from *downloads01.smarttech.com/media/sitecore/en/pdf/research_library/language_arts/the_digital_whiteboard_as_a_tool_in_increasing_student_attention_during_early_literacy_instruction.pdf.*

Spandel, V. (2007). *Creating young writers: Using the six traits to enrich the writing process in primary classrooms* (2nd ed.). New York: Addison Wesley Longman.

Spandel, V. (2008). *Creating writers through 6-trait writing assessment and instruction.* Boston: Allyn & Bacon.

Stauffer, R. (1969). *Directing reading maturity as a cognitive process.* New York: Harper & Row.

Stepp, L. S. (2000). *Our last best shot: Guiding our children through early adolescence.* New York: Riverhead Books.

Stevenson, R. L. (2001). *The strange case of Dr. Jekyll and Mr. Hyde.* New York: Scholastic. (Original work published 1886)

Steward, F., Golf, D., & Harris, S. (2007). Parent involvement enhances emergent literacy. *Illinois Reading Council Journal, 36*(1), 40–43.

Stotsky, S. (2006, January). *Whose literacy is declining?* Retrieved August 27, 2010, from *www.ednews.org/articles/whose-literacy-is-declining-new-frontiers-for-classroom-research-.html.*

Sullivan, M. (2009). *Connecting boys with books 2: Closing the reading gap.* Chicago: American Library Association.

Sylwester, R. (1995). *A celebration of neurons: An educator's guide to the human brain.* Alexandria, VA: Association for Supervision and Curriculum Development.

Sylwester, R. (1998). How emotions affect learning. In R. Sylwester (Ed.), *Student brains, school issues: A collection of articles* (pp. 29–39). Arlington Heights, IL: Skylight Professional Development.

Tate, M. L. (2003). *Worksheets don't grow dendrites.* Thousand Oaks, CA: Corwin Press.

Tatum, A. W. (2000). Breaking down barriers that disenfranchise African American adolescent readers in low-level tracks. *Journal of Adolescent and Adult Literacy, 44,* 52–64.

Tatum, A. W. (2009). *Reading for their life: (Re)building the textual lineages of African American adolescent males.* Portsmouth, NH: Heinemann.

Taylor, K., Marienau, C., & Fiddler, M. (2000). *Developing adult learners: Strategies for teachers and trainers.* San Francisco: Jossey-Bass.

Taylor, R. T. (2007). *Improving reading, writing, and content learning for students in grades 4–12.* Thousand Oaks, CA: Corwin Press.

Trelease, J. (2006). *The new read-aloud handbook* (5th ed.). New York: Penguin.

Tomlinson, C. (1999). *The differentiated classroom: Responding to the needs of all learners.* Alexandria, VA: Association for Supervision and Curriculum Development.

Tompkins, G. E. (2010). *Literacy in the 21st century.* Boston: Pearson Allyn & Bacon.

Tyre, P. (2008). *The trouble with boys: A surprising report card on our boys, their problems at school, and what parents and educators must do.* New York: Crown.

U.S. Census. (2000). *Castro Valley demographics.* Retrieved September 30, 2009, from *castrovalley.areaconnect.com/statistics.htm.*

Vellutino, F. R., Fletcher, J. M., Snowling, M. J., & Scanlon, D. M. (2004). Specific reading disability (dyslexia): What have we learned in the past four decades? *Journal of Child Psychology and Psychiatry, 45*(1), 2–40.

von Glasersfeld, E. (1996). Introduction: Aspects of constructivism. In C. T. Fosnot (Ed.), *Constructivism: Theory, perspectives, and practice* (pp. 3–7). New York: Teachers College Press.

Vygotsky, L. S. (1978). *Mind in society.* Cambridge, MA: Harvard University Press.

Walker, H. M., Ramsey, E., & Gresham, F. M. (2004). *Antisocial behavior in school: Evidence-based practices* (2nd ed.) Belmont, CA: Wadsworth/Thomson Learning.

Wegner, E. (2009). A social theory of learning. In K. Illeris (Ed.), *Contemporary theories of learning: In their own words* (pp. 209–218). London: Routledge.

White, E. B. (1952). *Charlotte's web.* New York: HarperCollins.

Whitehurst, G. J., & Lonigan, C. J. (1998). Examination of the relative efficacy of parent and teacher involvement in a shared-reading intervention for preschool children from low-income backgrounds. *Early Childhood Research Quarterly, 17,* 265–292.

Wilson, N. T. (1976). *St. Charles parish: A brief look at the past.* Retrieved November 28, 2010, from *www.stcharlesgov.net/index.aspx?page=915.*

Wisker, G., Exley, K., Antoniou, M., & Ridley, P. (2008). *Working one-to-one with students: Supervising, coaching, mentoring, and personal tutoring.* New York: Routledge.

Wlodkowski, R. J. (2004). Creating motivating learning environments. In M. W. Galbraith (Ed.), *Adult learning methods: A guide for effective instruction* (3rd ed., pp. 141–164). Malabar, FL: Krieger.

Wren, S. (2003). *What does a "balanced approach" to reading instruction mean?* Retrieved September 8, 2009, from *www.balancedreading.com/balanced.html.*

Yep, L. (1995). *Thief of hearts.* New York: HarperCollins.

Zambo, D., & Brozo, W. G. (2009). *Bright beginnings for boys: Engaging young boys in active literacy.* Newark, DE: International Reading Association.

Index

f following a page number indicates a figure; *t* following a page number indicates a table.